Humanism, Empire, and Nation
KOREAN LITERARY AND CULTURAL CRITICISM

Humanism, Empire, and Nation

Korean Literary and Cultural Criticism

Edited and Translated by

Travis Workman

Modern Language Association of America

New York   2023

To order MLA publications, visit www.mla.org/books. For wholesale and
international orders, see www.mla.org/bookstore-orders.

The MLA office is located on the island known as Mannahatta
(Manhattan) in Lenapehoking, the homeland of the Lenape people. The
MLA pays respect to the original stewards of this land and to the diverse
and vibrant Native communities that continue to thrive in New York
City.

Cover illustration: Kim Whanki, *Tranquility 5-IV-73 #310*, 1973.
© Whanki Foundation·Whanki Museum.

Texts and Translations 40

ISSN 1079-2538

Library of Congress Cataloging-in-Publication Data

Name: Workman, Travis, 1979- editor, translator.
Title: Humanism, empire, and nation: Korean literary and cultural
    criticism / edited and translated by Travis Workman.
Description: New York : Modern Language Association of America,
    2023. | Series: Texts and translations, 1079-2538 ; 40 | Simultaneously
    published in Korean as Hyumŏnijŭm, cheguk, minjok: Han'guk ŭi
    munhak kwa munhwa pip'yŏng. | Includes bibliographical references.
    | Identifiers: LCCN 2022049789 (print) | LCCN 2022049790 (ebook) |
    ISBN 9781603296120 (paperback) | ISBN 9781603296137 (EPUB)
Subjects: LCSH: Criticism—Korea—History—20th century. | Korean
    literature—20th century—History and criticism. | Literature
    and society. | Korean essays—Translations into English. | BISAC:
    LITERARY COLLECTIONS / Essays | LITERARY CRITICISM /
    Asian / General | LCGFT: Literary criticism. | Essays.
Classification: LCC PL952.6 .H83 2023 (print) | LCC PL952.6 (ebook) |
    DDC 895.709/004—dc23/eng/20221129
LC record available at https://lccn.loc.gov/2022049789
LC ebook record available at https://lccn.loc.gov/2022049790

CONTENTS

INTRODUCTION

Japan's colonization of Korea between 1910 and 1945 began
a twentieth century marked by extreme violence, dictatorial
political control, rapid social and economic change, and a per-
sistent feeling of crisis on the Korean peninsula. The effects
of Japanese colonialism reverberated throughout the Cold
War and up to the present, both politically and in the ways
that literary and cultural texts imagined the relationship between the Korean nation and the world. Although the Korean
War, from 1950 to 1953, remains the most defining geopol-
itical event for contemporary Korea, as the historian Bruce
Cumings showed, the conditions of the outbreak of that war
were not limited to the division of the peninsula along the
thirty-eighth parallel or to the US and Soviet military occupations, but included the class relations, political ideologies, and
economic crises that emerged through the Japanese colonial
system and its sudden collapse (xix–100). Furthermore, for
those who lived through the middle of the twentieth century
in Korea, the rapid succession of cataclysmic events was not
experienced as dates in a historical chronology but rather as

rapid transformations of everyday life that carried with them the effects and memories of the past, as well as dramatic breaks and discontinuities.

However, in the presentation of Korean literary and cultural history, there has been a tendency to think of the colonial period and the post-1945 Korean peninsula as distinct spaces and times disconnected by the chronological passage from one political system (under imperial Japan) to multiple others: US occupation (1945–present) of the South and Soviet occupation (1945–48) of the North, the Republic of Korea (South Korea, founded in 1948), and the Democratic People's Republic of Korea (North Korea, founded in 1948). The division of modern Korean literary and cultural studies according to these political sovereignties is an effect of the Cold War system and the desire to create singular and continuous national stories of liberation from Japanese colonialism in both North Korea and South Korea. However, the formative period of the mid–twentieth century that this book addresses was obviously experienced differently than what we see in a historical chronology. When we read, translate, and interpret the cultural and literary texts of modern Korea, we find both continuity and change, both repetition and difference across space and time. These continuities and changes exist in the social and cultural criticism concerning humanism, empires, nations, aesthetics, and society, as well as in the genres, styles, and voices of literary texts. To contribute to the effort of reading modern Korean-language texts of literary and cultural criticism across the typical chronological periodization of Korean history, and the spatial division between North and South, this volume brings together works written before and after 1945 from colonial Korea, South Korea, and North Korea. Rather than aiming for a cohesive national story, it is organized thematically around the question of what role humanist ideas played in the formation of national, imperial, and world literatures and cultures during the mid–twentieth century on the Korean peninsula.

By focusing specifically on humanist literary and cultural criticism, this volume is also intended to facilitate an exploration of how Korean critics have tried to situate modern Korean literature and culture within a broader story of human history and cultural creation, and therefore to open up Korean criticism and literature to comparison in its many modes. Although the meaning of literature, and especially national literature, transformed greatly in Korea between the colonial period and the Cold War, one important continuity was the humanist concern with how particular historical experiences and events relate to universal ideas about humanity and the human. The essays in this volume will, I hope, facilitate conversations about the endeavor of transforming what is local or national into something global and universal as well as about the social issues—including assimilation to imperialism, national subjectivity, capitalism, and state socialism—that emerge in this process. Since translation, especially from a local or national language into global English, is often understood to serve the function of bringing texts into a global context, reading these humanist texts in Korean and English also provides the opportunity to think about the difficulty of translation and how it may complicate our sense of how the local is connected to the global.

In thinking about these problems through humanist texts, readers should keep in mind that the human is not a natural category. Although we might presume to know commonsensically the meaning of the word *human* (인간; *in'gan*), the validity and value of various concepts of the human have been debated throughout modernity, including in modern Korea, and some philosophers, such as Michel Foucault, have argued that the human was not an object of knowledge at all until the modern era. In reading this volume, one should think about the human as a *figure*, meaning an image or concept that mediates between everyday experience and the abstract realm of ideas (Foucault 318). In these texts by Korean critics, the human appears against the background of defined historical and social contexts, such as empires, colonialism, nation building, and war. However, the human also represents an ideal, abstract form (or goal) of morality, knowledge, and education.

How, then, did the writers included here think about the figure of the human and its place in the modern world? How were their abstract interpretations of literary aesthetics and cultural forms related to global discussions of politics and society and questions of imperialism and national subjectivity? In the works of the critic Paik Ch'ŏl, we can trace how ideas about the so-called new human that were first articulated during the Japanese colonial period continued to affect how intellectuals understood the role of culture and literature in connecting the imagined national culture of South Korea to US empire and the larger world. Paik's work was pivotal because he was one of the first critics to explicitly introduce theoretical arguments about the human into literary criticism in Korea. Partially in response to anticommunism in Japan, South Korea, and the United States and partially through the development of his thinking, he frequently revised his early 1930s essays on human description, which originally advocated proletarian literature and socialist realism as ideal modes of human description. He eventually argued against both psychological literature (i.e., modernism) and proletarian literature, seeing them as two ways of failing to capture the living human in its historical periods—because psychological literature depicts a fragmented and internal human and because proletarian literature is too tied to an ideological and abstract economic theory ("In'gan myosaron"). Paik remained a leading figure in literary criticism and engaged with North American and European trends, such as New Criticism. Even in the aftermath of the devastation of the Korean War, he continued to argue for a literature that could help to create a new human who would enact the reconstruction of society and overcome the fragmentation that had been caused by imperialist capitalist expansion and colonial civil war.

In addition to their own distinct insights into world history, ethics, literature, and nostalgia, the works of Sŏ Insik included here provide a window into how ideas translated from the German context, such as from the works of G. W. F. Hegel, Karl Marx, and Martin Heidegger, and from Japan's so-called Kyoto school of philosophy, such as from the works of Nishida Kitarō, Kōyama Iwao, and Tanabe Hajime, affected how colonial Korean philosophers and critics imagined the role of literature and culture in integrating the colonized Korean nation into the greater Japanese Empire, the region of East Asia, and, most important for Sŏ, world history. Sŏ began publishing as part of the Marxist-Leninist Group, which developed cultural and philosophical criticisms of capitalism and Japanese imperialism, and his work can be situated within the rich period of global Hegelian-Marxist thought in the early twentieth century, particularly in the German traditions of philosophy and critical theory and in modern Japanese philosophy. However, after experiencing imprisonment and the political pressure of the anticommunist Japanese state, Sŏ eventually wrote favorably about the potential of the East Asian Community (동아공동체; *Tonga kongdongch'e*). Although his ideas about the East Asian Community cannot be entirely disentangled from Japan's imperial state project in the late 1930s and early 1940s, Ch'a Sŭnggi and Chŏng Chonghyŏn have argued convincingly that Sŏ asserted a humanist universalism that expressed ambivalence about whether the Japanese state could truly overcome ethnocentrism and the remnants of feudalism. Sŏ's case is paradigmatic for how the philosophies of world history at the end of the Japanese Empire facilitated the intellectual capitulation of some Marxists to political positions that were much less oppositional to Japan's imperialist expansion. We also see many ripple effects of Sŏ's type of dialectical and idealist mode of analysis and his discussions of the East Asian Community in many postliberation works in both North Korea and South Korea. At the same time, it is important to remember that Sŏ's universalist philosophy expressed skepticism about whether the Japanese state was up to the task of representing East Asian peoples in the arena of world history.

Ŏm Hosŏk's essay "The Problem of Typicality in Literary Composition" ("문학 창작에 있어서의 전형성의 문제"; "Munhak ch'angjak e issŏsŏ ŭi chŏnhyŏngsŏng ŭi munje"), from 1954, gives us a sense of how Paik's centering of the human, Sŏ's analysis of the dialectics of literary convention, and Ch'oe Chaesŏ's concern with cultivation were echoed in the state socialist literary criticism forming north of the demilitarized zone in North Korea. The essay also illustrates how seemingly innocent and apolitical humanist concepts of cultivation, morality, personality, and typology can be used to denounce and justify the execution or imprisonment of intellectuals, in this case, during the post–Korean War purges of 1953, when Kim Il Sung and his supporters in the Korean Workers' Party and the cultural sphere were consolidating their power over North Korean society and looking ahead to national reconstruction.

Finally, in the works of Ch'oe, a scholar of English literature, we can ask how and why an intellectual who engaged critically with the literature and philosophies of European modernism turned, like many of his counterparts in Europe, to fascist ideas about politics and aesthetics in supporting the program for a multiethnic Japanese national literature in the early 1940s. We can also see that many of his more disconcerting ideas about politics from that period were connected to his general understanding and theory of literature, which were indebted to well-known figures of English letters such as the Romantics, T. S. Eliot, and I. A. Richards, all of whom remained significant for the theories of literature that he articulated in South Korea under US neocolonial occupation. In the late 1930s he asserted that the cultivation and aesthetic education of the human were key to overcoming the fragmentation and alienation caused by modern society and culture, an idea that he overtly militarized and mobilized for the state in the late Japanese Empire and that continued to influence his canonical work on English literature and literary theory in the 1950s.

Excluding Ŏm, who does not seem to have collaborated with Japanese colonial authorities or made public statements in support of Japan, Paik, Sŏ, and Ch'oe would all have been labeled pro-Japanese (친일; *ch'inil*) in a strict application of the Cold War framework of national liberation and national subjectivity. In the early 1940s, these three critics wrote favorably, although to varying degrees and from different political positions, of the possibilities of a Japan-led Korea and East Asia, and Paik and Ch'oe published numerous articles in Japanese. However, just as the desire for the chronological marker of 1945 to represent an absolute break from colonization to liberation led to an obscuring of how the period was experienced in everyday cultural life and represented in literary texts, understanding the cultural politics of mid–twentieth century Korea in terms of pro- and anti-Japanese positions does little to explain how and why the humanist discourses of the late Japanese Empire might repeat in a different form in the postwar attempts to form a Korean national culture and literature. One main purpose of this volume, in addition to making important texts of Korean criticism available to readers of English, is to open up these political conundrums to properly comparative methodologies in research and in the classroom, and therefore to move beyond simplistic readings that are dependent on Cold War national identities and political oppositions.

I would now like to provide some brief context and interpretation to facilitate the reading of these texts. Paik's "The
Era of Human Description" ("인간묘사시대"; "In'gan myosa
sidae") in many ways inaugurated the debates on humanism that would have a prominent place in Korean literary
criticism throughout the rest of the twentieth century. Influenced by socialist realism and later the humanism prominent
among European liberals in the 1930s, Paik sought a theory
of literary representation that would bridge elite and popular literatures and not reduce human characters to isolated
psychological individuals. He directs his criticism toward the
bourgeois psychological literature, including the works of
now canonical authors of European modernism such as Marcel Proust and James Joyce. He ends the essay with a call for
socialist realism, only a year after it was officially established
as the aesthetic system of the Soviet Union, stating that it offers a path toward describing the human as a living and social
being. In later revisions of this essay, and following debates
with members of Korea Artista Proleta Federacio (KAPF; the
Korean Federation of Proletarian Artists), Paik came to criticize leftist literature for its propensity to reduce human characters to symbols acting unrealistically and without free will,
according to an abstract political or economic theory ("In'gan
myosaron").[1] I have transcribed and translated the original essay directly from *The Chosun Ilbo* (조선일보; *Chosŏn ilbo*) articles
of 1933. However, I encourage teachers and students to compare this version with the versions that appear in *The Complete
Literary Works of Paik Ch'ŏl* (백철문학전집; *Paik Ch'ŏl munhak
chŏnjip*) and in *The Selected Criticism of Paik Ch'ŏl* (백철평론선집;

Paik Ch'ŏl p'yŏngnon sŏnjip). Comparison of the different versions reveals how Paik later expanded his criticisms of mechanistic representations of the human to include leftist literary movements, arguing that they simplify humans and human action according to an abstract economic theory. In later versions he also quotes a more conservative source on humanism, John Ruskin, and compares the formation of human subjectivity through literary description to the "sculpting" of a Buddha statue ("조상"; "chosang"; "In'gan myosaron" 38). As he revised the essay, he began to turn to the humanism of the International Congress for the Defense of Culture, held in Paris in 1935, rather than to Soviet socialist realism.[2] Comparing the original 1933 text with the revisions reveals a fascinating historical palimpsest reflecting the political pressures directed toward leftist critics in the late Japanese Empire and in South Korea, as well as Paik's changing ideas about the possibility of proletarian literature to capture the spirit and social conditions of the human.

In each version of Paik's humanism in the essay, his primary concern is to understand human description as involved in the human's active formation and to argue against treating the human as an isolated, mechanical individual lacking in consciousness or sociality. His idea for the description of human types aims to improve on existing versions of realism by creating characters who embody both the spirit and the material social conditions of an era. Against both naturalist description and psychological literature, which cannot capture the living human, he sides with the so-called tendentious literature of European socialists such as Friedrich

Engels and Minna Kautsky, as well as Korea's early leftist literary organization, the New Tendency Group (신경향파; *Sin'gyŏnghyangp'a*).[3] He argues that tendentious literature can describe the human as something more than a mechanical historical actor, as a being with free will and purpose.

In the early 1940s, Paik wrote articles in Japanese about the possibility of a multiethnic Japanese national literature that would include Korean literature as a minority literature. However, after the end of the Pacific War and liberation from Japanese colonial rule, he applied a similar liberal humanist vision of national literature to the development of a Korean-language national literature that would appeal to the popular masses (대중; *taejung*). One primary concern of "Literature for Thirty Million Koreans: What Kind of Literature Do the People Desire?" ("삼천만인의 문학—민중은 어떤 문학을 요망하는가"; "Samch'ŏnman in ŭi munhak—minjung ŭn ŏttŏn munhak ŭl yomang hanŭn'ga"), published one month before the start of the Korean War, is how writers can meet the challenge of connecting with a sophisticated mass audience for art. According to Paik, with the reemergence of the possibility of a Korean-language national literature, the reading public desires and is prepared to encounter a literature that speaks to their experiences and the actuality of their daily lives, but the writers have failed to advance adequately. In the essay, Paik searches for a popular and public literature without the abstract, top-down "popularization" ("대중화"; "taejunghwa") in the mode of proletarian writers and without a condescending and pandering reliance on sensational and vulgar imagery.[4] He seeks a "pure literature" ("순수 문학"; "sunsu munhak") that captures the complexity of the living human while also being popular. Read retrospectively, the essay ends on a tragic note, as Paik states his hope that with the future reunification of Korea his idea for a humanist popular literature would come to fruition and connect all the Korean people, something that would soon be rendered impossible by the circumstances of the Korean War.

Paik's critiques of naturalism in "What Comes after Naturalism: The Unity of the External Human and the Psychological World" ("자연주의 뒤에 올 것—외적 인간과 심리계의 통일"; "Chayŏnjuŭi ŭi twi e ol kŏt—oejŏk in'gan kwa simnigye ŭi t'ongil") were in many ways a continuation of the project he began two decades earlier during the colonial period: to develop a literature that does not simply describe empirically but rather shows the living human in its process of becoming a subject and unifying with the objects of ethics and knowledge. Looking back to the International Congress for the Defense of Culture, Paik tries in the essay to revitalize the antifascist and liberal humanism of that period without expressing his earlier explicit support of socialist realism. Looking ahead, and despite the fact that the devastating Korean War had ended only three years earlier, Paik maintains hope that a new literature developed creatively and autonomously by Korean writers can contribute to the construction of a new human as part of the educational and governmental project of forming new national subjects who are capable of rebuilding South Korean society (a theme echoed in Ŏm's postwar text from North Korea). It may seem untimely that Paik maintains such optimism for the humanist project in the aftermath of such cataclysmic violence, but his returning to the human as the being that can unite the past of tradition with the future of national literature shows the power of humanist ideas.

The volume includes three essays by Sŏ, one of the most erudite philosophers and critics of the late 1930s and early 1940s. These essays were all published in 1940 and were chosen because of the insight they provide into the humanist philosophical and critical foundations of the discourses of East Asian Community in the late Japanese Empire. In "The Idea and Form of Eastern Culture: Its Particularity and Generality" ("동양문화의 이념과 형태—그 특수성과 일반성"; "Tong-yang munhwa ŭi inyŏm kwa hyŏngt'ae—kŭ t'ŭksusŏng kwa ilbansŏng") we can see the appropriation of a Hegelian mapping of world history, self-consciousness, and reason according to the geographical fallacies of East and West, through the translation and interpretation of statements of major philosophers of the time, such as Nishida and Kōyama. According to Sŏ, there are fundamental differences between Eastern culture and Western culture, including a lack in Eastern culture that has prevented it from acting as a unified subject in world history, from applying consistent scientific logic and reason to the "Being" ("존재"; "chonjae") of phenomena, or asserting a universal "Idea" ("이데아"; "idea") of community. He takes up and elaborates on Nishida's discussions of subjectivity as "acting intuition" ("行為的直感"; "행위적 직관"; "haengwijŏk chikkwan") and Nishida's philosophy of absolute "nothingness" ("무"; "mu"), as well as Kōyama's categorical opposition between East and West in the context of a philosophy of world history (see Nishida).

"The Idea and Form of Eastern Culture" shows that for many Korean intellectuals, particularly a former Marxist-Leninist like Sŏ, the idea of the East Asian Community could not be founded on an existing religious or philosophical tradition with Asian origins, such as Confucianism, Buddhism, or Taoism. For Sŏ these traditions remain tied to the particularity of their national contexts and are characterized by a negation of the world and an ascetic ethos that prevent them from becoming foundational for a continuous and unifying Eastern tradition of knowledge and practice. Japan-centered pan-Asianism is commonly thought to be based in revivalist ideologies that critiqued Western modernity and argued for a return to Asian traditions. However, contrary to typical assumptions about the Asian religious and philosophical foundations for Japanese imperialist ideology in the 1940s, this essay shows that it was often secular humanism and its power in the modern world that coded how imperial intellectuals imagined the lack of subjectivity, but also future possibilities, in Eastern culture. For example, much of the work on Nishida and the Kyoto school of philosophy, both of which influenced Sŏ greatly, assumes that their Japan-centered pan-Asianism was a religious ideology and that their philosophical notions of nothingness and their support for the Japanese state were both traceable to the influence of Zen Buddhism (see Heisig and Maraldo). Sŏ's essay shows that modern philosophy across East Asia at the time was too complex to be accounted for by a single religious or cultural tradition and that a translated version of European humanism perhaps provided the most powerful intellectual justification for assimilation to the idea of East

Asian Community. Finally, this essay shows how philosophers such as Sŏ translated into Korea the distinction in Japanese philosophy between the epistemological subject (주관; *chugwan*) of scientific observation and the practical subject (주체; *chuch'e*) of moral and political action. In addition to being central to Sŏ's theories of culture and literature, the idea that appears in this essay that the practical human subject is the embodiment of world-historical action and development would go on to influence Juche thought (주체사상; *chuch'e sasang*) in North Korea and other political theories of the Cold War.

In "Literature and Ethics" ("문학과 윤리"; "Munhak kwa yulli"), Sŏ turns his concern with the power of ideas in culture and politics to literature and the ethical limitations of literary works that merely describe existing conventions and conditions. As a former communist, Sŏ held a concept of community that seems ostensibly at odds with Paik's liberal humanist and Ch'oe's fascist ideas, but he was in many ways building on their work. Sŏ cites Paik's and Ch'oe's criticisms of modern psychological literature in "Literature and Ethics" and shares these writers' concern with a lack of ethics and humanism in contemporary literature, and he ends the essay with a direct reference to Ch'oe's "The Expansion and Deepening of Realism" in calling for "human ethical authenticity" ("인간적 윤리적 진실"; "in'ganjŏk yullijŏk chinsil") as the guiding principle for realism (see also Ch'oe, "Riarijŭm" and "Expansion"). However, in a complex and dialectical reading of the relationship between convention and freedom in the ethics of literature, he argues that a genuine literature would represent existing conditions and conventions at the same time as it accounts for human freedom and emotions that exist beyond any particular historical moment. Just as Eastern culture required both particularity and generality to accede to the level of world history, literature for Sŏ is both immersed in the particular ethical conventions of discrete historical moments, which he refers to with the German term *Gemüt*, meaning mind or feeling, and aspires toward a moral universality that transcends particular conditions, which he refers to as *Sitte*, or customs. The purpose of literature and its participation in the transformation of society is to reconcile the transhistorical idea of truth with the moral authenticity of particular historical actors through a genuine representation of humanness. Again, the figure of the human is asked to serve the role as the ultimate mediation between the grand ideas that drive history and particular historical situations. Sŏ's materialist criticism of capitalism and culture has in "Literature and Ethics" given way to a newfound idealist view of the ethics of literature that is in some respects resonant with the theorizations of imperial Japanese literature by critics such as Ch'oe; although, again, Sŏ tends toward universalist arguments that can also be read as implicit criticisms of Japanese ethnonationalism.

Sŏ's "Sociology of Nostalgia" ("'향수'의 사회학"; "'Hyangsu' ŭi sahoehak") concerns one of the most pressing issues in literary and cultural criticism of the Japanese Empire, which is the modern subject's connection to "home," my translation of "고향" ("kohyang") in Sŏ's essay. During an era of ultranationalism and the revival of tradition in fascist states, the question of how to analyze critically the widespread desire for a return to origins was an essential one for those Marxists who sought to maintain a more rational critique of modern capitalist society, as well as for liberal advocates of multiethnic empire who saw that an overly ethnocentric view of origins could be detrimental to the assimilation of minorities and colonial subjects. There were also unexpected twists in the reading of "home" and its connection to origins, such as the case of Im Hwa, the former leader of KAPF, whom one would expect to remain critical of the romantic and nostalgic view of home in fascist writings. As part of his support for the idea of a Japan-led East Asia, Im argued that the peasant literature of Japan should express a nostalgic view of the home village (also *kohyang*) that could provide a unified vision of origins for all East Asians (Im, "Ilbon nongmin"). In "Sociology of Nostalgia," Sǒ intervenes into the contentious discussion of home by analyzing the ideological and existential aspects of nostalgia (향수; *hyangsu*), a word that both in Korean and English (or Greek) refers to a strong feeling of pathos for home, especially an unfulfilled desire to return. By developing a more universal analysis of nostalgia that includes a theoretical explication of its ideological and commonsense interpretations, as well as the conceptualization of the human's general uncanny exile from a "primal home" ("원시고향"; "wǒnsi kohyang"), Sǒ unmoors the problem of nostalgia from any particular idea of origin in a nationalist ideology and addresses the fundamental existential anxieties that lead to nostalgia in modernity.

As discussed above, Ǒm's "The Problem of Typicality in Literary Composition" is an example of how humanist ideas concerning the cultivation of the human for the purposes of nation building can be found not only in colonial

Korea and South Korea but also in the state socialist society of North Korea. The North Korean state was formed
out of a Manchuria-based partisan movement against Japanese colonialism in the 1930s and was led until 1994 by one
leader of that partisan movement, Kim Il Sung. Despite the
anti-Japanese credentials of North Korean state leadership
throughout the Cold War, however, Ŏm's essay is an example
of how discussions of the centrality of cultivation (교양; *kyoyang*) for modernization and nation building that go back to
Meiji-era Japan were echoed in very early critical discussions
of North Korean–style socialist realism.

Socialist realism was a style of literature and the arts developed in the Soviet Union in the early 1930s by leading Russian
artists such as Maxim Gorky, who claimed that this aesthetic
system would document the socialist state's revolutionary
transformation of social reality through a combination of
realism and Romanticism. Although socialist realism was
certainly known by leftist intellectuals in colonial Korea, and
Paik's "The Era of Human Description" mentions it favorably,
the fully developed theories and practices of socialist realism
were translated into the North Korean context during the Soviet occupation of the territory in the aftermath of World War
II. With Gorky's addition of Romanticism to critical realism's
call to describe the economic and political exploitation of the
capitalist system, we get some sense of how postrevolution-
ary socialist literatures were also concerned with the cultivation of human subjects through the reformation of their will
and imagination. Therefore, Ŏm's primary political concern
with the cultivation of the popular masses is based to some

degree on socialist realism itself, but I would argue that Ŏm is also very much in conversation with the other strains of humanist thinking traced in this volume. He repeats some central tenets of socialist realism, such as the requirement that literature portray the "positive protagonists" ("긍정적 주인공"; "kŭngjŏngjŏk chuin'gong") of the socialist revolution, and writes of shaping the "noble moral character" ("고상한 도덕적 품성"; "kosanghan todŏkchŏk p'umsŏng") of subjects and instilling in them "good intentions, keen wisdom, active will, and so on" ("선량한 지향, 밝은 지혜, 적극적 의지 등"; "sŏllyanghan chihyang, palgŭn chihye, chŏkkŭkchŏk ŭiji tŭng")—qualities that each of the essays in the volume, from the political left or right, also sees as the necessary effect of cultivation. Ŏm calls for the purging from the party of the great critics and writers Im, Yi T'aejun, and Kim Namch'ŏn and a return to the "core" ("핵심적"; "haeksimjŏk") writers of KAPF. Although Im led KAPF in the early 1930s, he was blamed for its dissolution in 1935 under great pressure from the Japanese state, and in this essay Ŏm accuses him—falsely, we can assume—of being an American spy. The appearance of proper human cultivation as the central concept of such a denunciation shows how universal humanist claims can often be put in the service of masking or legitimating illogical or immoral political positions. The essay also provides some of the prehistory to the human-centered philosophy of Juche thought, which would eventually become official North Korean policy in the late 1960s.

Another troubling intersection of humanism and politics appears in the works of Ch'oe. As discussed above, Ch'oe's early 1930s criticisms of the fragmentation of subjectivity in psychological literature, particularly in the works of modernist authors such as Proust, Joyce, and Yi Sang, as well as his search for a moral basis for literary subjectivity, were extremely influential throughout mid-century Korea. Against fragmentation and with an eye toward reintegrating human experience into a coherent whole through aesthetic education and cultivation, Ch'oe published "The Spirit of Cultivation" ("교양의 정신"; "Kyoyang ŭi chŏngsin") in the cosmopolitan journal *Humanities Critique* (인문평론; *Inmun p'yŏngnon*). Ch'oe states in the essay that cultivation and culture are not simply matters of individual education and development, but rather cultivation brings the individual into the life of the whole of society, and therefore cultivation must be a matter of both the individual and the whole. To contrast his ideas of education and cultivation with mere occupational training, he relies on the classic contrast between organic bodies and mechanisms, a contrast first expressed in German idealism, then in English letters by Matthew Arnold, and then in the works of Yi Kwangsu, who called for a cultural rather than mechanical education for the Korean nation as early as 1917 (Fichte; Arnold 37; Yi 328). Although Ch'oe's idea of community as an organic body was a central metaphor for the nation in fascist culture during this period, Ch'oe makes a significant plea for an education that exposes students to heterogeneous and foreign phenomena that are then brought into a harmonious state through collective cultivation.

In "What Is Poetic?" ("何が詩的であるか"; "Nani ga shiteki de aru ka"), a section of a Japanese-language book of criticism that Ch'oe published at the height of the Pacific War, *Korean Literature in a Time of Transition* (転換期の朝鮮文学; *Tenkanki no Chōsen bungaku*), we can see how the cosmopolitan idea of cultivation in the 1939 essay transformed into a more overt Japanese imperial nationalism. In the early 1940s, *Humanities Critique* became *National Literature* (国民文学; *Kokumin bungaku*), a mostly Japanese-language journal that advocated that Korean writers write as much as possible in the national language (Japanese) and that they participate in the creation of a new, multiethnic Japanese national literature. In addition to Ch'oe's references to Japanese literary traditions, and traditional works such as the *Man'yōshū* (万葉集; *Collection of Ten Thousand Leaves*),[5] as the foundation for this imperial-national literature, the essay also includes repetitions of the more general themes found in Ch'oe's "The Spirit of Cultivation," particularly in the idea that the individual is integrated into the organic whole through cultural, moral, and political practices (such as when children of a national school march in file, guided by a single idea). Furthermore, the essay argues, it is not through a social contract or shared laws that an ideal society is formed, but rather through an aesthetic experience of beauty on the part of both the participants in a mass formation and the onlooker. Such an image of total immersion in the beautiful whole belongs identifiably to fascist aesthetics, and through a comparison between "The Spirit of Cultivation" and "What Is Poetic?," it becomes possible to trace some of the uncomfortable connections between the humanist idea of cultivation as an organic cultural process and the fascist political formation.

Finally, in "The Idea of Literature" ("문학의 이념"; "Mun-hak ŭi inyŏm"), from his postwar work *Literary Theory* (문학원론; *Munhak wŏllon*), Ch'oe argues in a different way for litera-ture as individual and collective expression and as a "valuable record of human experience" ("가치있는 인간적 체험의 기록"; "kach'i innŭn in'ganjŏk ch'ehŏm ŭi kirok"). His ability with languages and his erudition are reflected in how central he was to Korean scholarship on European modernism, Japanese literature, and English literature throughout the mid-century, and his ability in the translation and interpretation of canoni-cal texts in English literary criticism is well represented in *Lit-erary Theory*. However, in the context of US occupation and Korean ethnonationalism—very much defined against Japan prior to the normalization of South Korean–Japanese relations in the mid-1960s—he does not, in his postliberation works, reflect critically on how he had previously put his English and Japanese literary education to work for the Japanese Empire and fascism. He remained a right-wing stalwart during the Korean War, expressing his unwavering support for United States military leadership by writing *The MacArthur Sensation* (매카-더 선풍; *Maek'a-dŏ sŏnp'ung*) and by translating Frank Kelley and Cornelius Ryan's *MacArthur: Man of Action* (Ch'oe, *Yŏng'ung Maek'a-dŏ*; see also Chŏng 184–86). This career tra-jectory forces us to question the politics of literary form, and especially aesthetic concepts of organic expression, the beauty of war, and revitalized tradition, beyond the imperial and na-tional identities to which they are applied in a particular case. I will have fulfilled my purpose in translating and editing this volume if it helps teachers and students ask and discuss such questions, questions that demand a self-reflective thinking through of the interconnections in modernity between ideas of the human and the practices of empire and nation building and that do not allow us to rely on an inherited nationalism of the victim or the perpetrator in the catastrophic period of the mid–twentieth century.

Notes

1. KAPF was an influential proletarian arts organization in colonial Korea that existed between 1925 and its disbandment in 1935. Members of the group were subject to numerous arrests and censorship by Japan's colonial authorities.

2. The International Congress for the Defense of Culture was a meeting held at La Maison de Mutualité. It was attended by numerous luminaries of European letters, including André Malraux, André Gide, Robert Musil, Henri Barbusse, and Bertolt Brecht. The purpose of the meeting was to articulate a defense of culture and humanism in the face of war and the rise of fascism.

3. In the early twentieth century, *tendentious literature* referred to literature that had a political tendency, as opposed to art for art's sake, and was theorized by Kautsky, Engels, and other European Marxists. The New Tendency Group formed in colonial Korea in the early 1920s. It also criticized art for art's sake, including the famous short story writer Kim Tongin, and insisted that literature should address social, political, and economic issues such as poverty and colonialism. The New Tendency Group's writing was the first literature in Korea to engage explicitly in class politics and a critique of capitalism. It was a precursor to proletarian literature and KAPF.

4. Original-language quotations from Paik Ch'ŏl's "Literature for Thirty Million Koreans"; Sŏ Insik's "The Idea and Form of Eastern Culture," "Literature and Ethics," and "Sociology of Nostalgia"; Ŏm Hosŏk's "The Problem of Typicality in Literary Composition"; and Ch'oe Chaesŏ's "The Idea of Literature" are from the companion to this volume, published by the Modern Language Association of America in 2023.

5. The *Man'yōshū* is a collection of more than four thousand poems dating from eighth-century Japan. It is considered an important foundation for Japanese literature and was represented to Japan's colonial subjects in the 1930s and 1940s as a classic of imperial-national literature and the national language; see *Thousand Poems*.

Works Cited

Arnold, Matthew. *Culture and Anarchy*. Oxford UP, 2006.

Ch'a Sŭnggi and Chŏng Chonghyŏn. "한 보편주의자의 삶" ["Han pop'yŏnjuŭija ŭi sam"; "Life of a Universalist"]. 역사와 문화 [*Yŏksa wa munhwa*; *History and Culture*], by Sŏ Insik, edited by Ch'a and Chŏng, Yŏngnak, 2006, pp. 5–14. Vol. 1 of 서인식 전집 [*Sŏ Insik chŏnjip*; *Sŏ Insik Complete Works*].

Ch'oe Chaesŏ. "The Expansion and Deepening of Realism: On *Scenes by a Stream* and 'Wings.'" Translated by Christopher Hanscom. *Imperatives of Culture: Selected Essays from Korean History, Literature, and Society from the Japanese Colonial Period*, edited by Hanscom et al., U of Hawai'i P, 2013, pp. 165–79.

———. "교양의 정신" ["Kyoyang ŭi chŏngsin"; "The Spirit of Cultivation"]. 인문평론 [*Inmun p'yŏngnon*; *Humanities Critique*], vol. 2, Nov. 1939, pp. 24–29.

———. 매카-더 선풍 [*Maek'a-dŏ sŏnp'ung*; *The MacArthur Sensation*]. Hyanghaksa, 1951.

———. "문학의 이념" ["Munhak ŭi inyŏm"; "The Idea of Literature"]. 문학원론 [*Munhak wŏllon*; *Literary Theory*], Ch'unjosa, 1957, pp. 1–16.

———. "何が詩的であるか" ["Nani ga shiteki de aru ka"; "What Is Poetic?"]. 転換期の朝鮮文学 [*Tenkanki no Chōsen bungaku*; *Korean Literature in a Time of Transition*], Jinbunsha, 1943, pp. 181–86.

———. "리아리즘의 확대와 심화" ["Riarijŭm ŭi hwaktae wa simhwa"; "The Expansion and Deepening of Realism"]. 한국현대 모더니즘 비평선집 [*Han'guk hyŏndae modŏnijŭm pip'yong sŏnjip*; *Selected Works of Korean Modernist Criticism*], edited by Kim Yunsik, Seoul Taehakkyo Ch'ulp'anbu, 1988, pp. 161–71.

———, translator. 영웅 매카-더 장군전 [*Yŏngung Maek'a-dŏ changgunjŏn*; *Biography of the Hero General MacArthur*]. Ilsŏngdang, 1952.

Chŏng Chonghyŏn. "최재서의 '맥아더': 맥아더 표상을 통해 본 한 친일 엘리트의 해방전후 ["Ch'oe Chaesŏ ŭi 'Maegadŏ': Maegadŏ p'yosang ŭl t'onghae pon han ch'inil ellit'ŭ ŭi haebang chŏnhu"; "Ch'oe Chaesŏ's MacArthur: A Pro-Japanese Elite before and after Liberation Viewed through the Emblem of MacArthur"]. 동악어문학 [*Tongak ŏmunhak; Tongak Language and Literature*], no. 59, 2012, pp. 183–222.

Cumings, Bruce. *Liberation and the Emergence of Separate Regimes.* Princeton UP, 1981. Vol. 1 of *The Origins of the Korean War.*

Fichte, J. G. *Addresses to the German Nation.* Edited by Gregory Moore, Cambridge UP, 2006.

Foucault, Michel. *The Order of Things.* Translated by Alan Sheridan, Vintage Books, 1994.

Gorky, Maxim. "Soviet Literature." *Soviet Writers' Congress 1934: The Debate on Socialist Realism and Modernism in the Soviet Union*, edited by H. G. Scott, Lawrence and Wishart, 1977, pp. 27–70.

Heisig, James W., and John C. Maraldo, editors. *Rude Awakenings: Zen, the Kyoto School, and the Question of Nationalism.* U of Hawai'i P, 1995.

Im Hwa. "일본 농민 문학의 동향: 특히 '토의 문학'을 중심으로 ["Ilbon nongmin munhak ŭi tonghyang: T'ŭkhi 't'o ŭi munhak' ŭl chungsim ŭro"; "Tendencies in Japan's Peasant Literature: Particularly through 'Literature of the Land'"]. 문학의 논리 [*Munhak ŭi nolli; The Logic of Literature*], Somyŏng, 2009, pp. 630–43. Vol. 3 of 임화문학예술전집 [*Im Hwa munhak yesul chŏnjip; The Complete Literary Art of Im Hwa*].

Kelley, Frank, and Cornelius Ryan. *MacArthur: Man of Action.* Lion Books, 1951.

Nishida Kitarō. "行為的直感" ["Kōi-teki chokkan"; "Acting Intuition"]. 西田幾多郎全集 [*Nishida Kitarō zenshū; Nishida Kitarō Complete Works*], vol. 8, Iwanami, 1965, pp. 541–71.

Ŏm Hosŏk. "문학 창작에 있어서의 전형성의 문제" ["Munhak ch'angjak e issŏsŏ ŭi chŏnhyŏngsŏng ŭi munje"; "The Problem of Typicality in Literary Creation"]. 문학의 지향 [*Munhak ŭi chihyang; The Aims of Literature*], Chosŏn Chakka Tongmaeng, 1954, pp. 128–43.

Paik Ch'ŏl. "자연주의 뒤에 올 것—외적 인간과 심리계의 통일" ["Chayŏnjuŭi twi e ol kŏt—oejŏk in'gan kwa simnigye ŭi t'ongil"; "What Comes after Naturalism: The Unity of the External Human and the Psychological World"]. 문학예술 [*Munhak yesul; Literary Arts*], vol. 3, no. 1, 1956, pp. 116–22.

———. "인간묘사론" ["In'gan myosaron"; "On Human Description"]. Paik, 백철평론선집 [*Paik Ch'ŏl p'yŏngnon sŏnjip*], pp. 35–48.

———. "인간묘사시대" ["In'gan myosa sidae"; "The Era of Human Description"]. 조선일보 [*Chosŏn ilbo; The Chosun Ilbo*], 29 Aug.–1 Sept. 1933. *Chosun News Library*, newslibrary.chosun.com.

———. 백철문학전집 [*Paik Ch'ŏl munhak chŏnjip; The Complete Literary Works of Paik Ch'ŏl*]. Sin'gu Munhwasa, 1968. 4 vols.

———. 백철평론선집 [*Paik Ch'ŏl p'yŏngnon sŏnjip; The Selected Criticism of Paik Ch'ŏl*], edited by Yi Sŭngha, Chisik ŭl Mandŭnŭn Chisik, 2015.

———. "삼천만인의 문학—민중은 어떤 문학을 요망하는가" ["Samch'ŏnman in ŭi munhak—minjung ŭn ŏttŏn munhak ŭl yomang hanŭn'ga"; "Literature for Thirty Million Koreans: What Kind of Literature Do the People Desire?"]. 문학 [*Munhak; Literature*], May 1950, pp. 120–25.

Sŏ Insik. "'향수'의 사회학" ["'Hyangsu' ŭi sahoehak"; "Sociology of 'Nostalgia'"]. 조광 [*Chogwang; Morning Light*], vol. 6, no. 11, 1940, pp. 182–89.

———. "문학과 윤리" ["Munhak kwa yulli"; "Literature and Ethics"]. 인문평론 [*Inmun p'yŏngnon; Humanities Critique*], vol. 2, no. 10, 1940, pp. 6–22.

———. "동양문화의 이념과 형태—그 특수성과 일반성" ["Tongyang munhwa ŭi inyŏm kwa hyŏngt'ae—kŭ t'ŭksusŏng kwa ilbansŏng"; "The Idea and Form of Eastern Culture: Its Particularity and Generality"]. 동아일보 [*Tonga ilbo; The Dong-a Ilbo*], 3–12 Jan. 1940.

A Thousand Poems from the Manyōshū: The Complete Nippon Gakujutsu Shinkokai Translation. Translated by the Japanese Classics Translation Committee, Dover, 2005.

Yi Kwangsu. "신생활론" ["Sinsaenghwal lon"; "On the New Life"]. 이광수전집 [*Yi Kwangsu chŏnjip; Yi Kwangsu Complete Works*], vol. 10, Usinsa, 1979, pp. 325–51.

NOTE ON THE TRANSLATIONS

It is now widely accepted that no translation merely communicates or decodes a message in a source language and provides an equivalent version of that message in the target language. Such an idea of translation fails to recognize not only the internal transformations of the target language that are often necessary to translate well but also the historical and social differences between the space and time of the original and those of the translation.

In translating these works of modern Korean literary and cultural criticism, I have confronted each of these issues, but I also hope to have come to approximate solutions in most of the cases. Fortunately for my effort, the language of modern literary and cultural criticism in colonial Korea, South Korea, and North Korea is in many ways a language of modernity shared across the world. Each critic writes about some of modernity's major concepts: literature, history, society, morality, realism, social class, politics, nation, culture, and the human. In that sense, translation is facilitated by the shared vocabulary of modernity. On the other hand, there is no conceptual or semiotic equivalency between translations of the terms of modernity either. For example, in the first essay, "The Era of Human Description," Paik Ch'ŏl uses the term 인간 (*in'gan*) to refer to the human, and 인간학 (*in'ganhak*) to refer to philosophical anthropology or the study of the human. However, there are other words for the human that have a less specific meaning, such as 사람 (*saram*), and academic terms that connote ethnographic observation rather than philosophical inquiry, such as 인류학 (*illyuhak*). Although more convenient, translating *in'ganhak* as "anthropology" would elide the conceptual difference between the field of *in'ganhak* in Korea and East Asia more broadly and the field of anthropology as Anglophones would commonly understand it (*illyuhak*). This risk of elision is suggested by Paik himself, who adds the modifier "philosophical" to his first use of *in'ganhak* in the essay. Therefore, despite the seeming transparency provided by the terms of modernity, these terms tend to show, in translation, an opacity, to use a term of Édouard Glissant's, that the practice of translation cannot entirely overcome. There has been no easy solution to some of these incongruences, except to mark and explain my choices and to provide glosses in the endnotes to the essays. In this case, I have followed Paik's suggestion and translated *in'ganhak* throughout as "philosophical anthropology."

A similar opacity pertains to differences in Korean in the use of tenses, subject and object designation, transitive and intransitive verbs, and linguistic conventions of academic style. Because of the distance between Korean and English, in each of these cases, I have tried to maintain the semantic meaning of the original while deemphasizing strict adherence to syntactic construction, except when the semantics, connotation, or mood of a passage is tied intimately to an idiosyncratic syntax. Because these critics' works are so allusive and erudite, one big challenge was to capture the subtle connotations and interpretations in their readings of other works. To facilitate presenting their interpretations clearly, I have made extensive use of original English texts and accepted translations of texts that they quote, particularly European and classical East Asian texts for which standard and accepted editions in English exist.

The issue of historicity is more difficult to convey in the translations themselves, and I have attempted to show the significance and context of the essays and their arguments in the introduction to the volume and the endnotes to the essays. Questions concerning the tone and position of the pieces, as in Paik Ch'ŏl's critiques of both modernism and proletarian literature in the opening essay, are difficult to answer without knowing the backdrop of movements and debates into which the essays are intervening. I have tried to keep this historicity of the original texts in mind in my own language use and to capture how each critic attempts to situate himself in relation to his historical moment, as he sees it. I have also tried to highlight as much as possible the unique perspective and conceptual framework offered by each essay, to maintain through precision in translation a respect for modern Korea's traditions of literary and cultural theory.

As an editor, I chose texts with the intention of tracing continuities between the Japanese Empire and the Cold War era and presenting a variety of humanist positions on literature and culture. I also have more basic pedagogical reasons for choosing to translate these particular texts and to publish the translations and originals in companion volumes. As more and more texts of Korean fiction and poetry are translated into English, it has become gradually easier to teach courses in English translation and to approach more difficult literary texts in upper-level Korean language courses. In contrast to fiction and poetry, however, fewer texts of Korean criticism, philosophy, or theory have appeared in English translation. As in all other national literatures, modern Korean fiction and poetry influenced and were influenced by critical essays that address how particular literary aesthetics and styles are connected to broader social and epistemological issues and debates. Not only is it useful to be able to read literary and cultural criticism along with fiction and poetry texts, but these essays also provide an excellent introduction to the vocabulary and constructions of academic Korean. Although the language and references in these texts are not entirely contemporary, through them students can begin to have a solid foundation in reading advanced texts in the Korean humanities and social sciences. I have used the McCune-Reischauer romanization system throughout, except when convention dictates otherwise.

The endnotes to the essays indicate the versions of original texts in Korean and Japanese that I used for translation. I have used original newspaper articles, journal articles, and books whenever possible. For pedagogical purposes, I have updated some Korean spelling, punctuation, and romanizations to fit contemporary standards. In a couple of cases, I have resorted to using versions of essays collected in later anthologies, which can reflect minor revisions made by the authors or editors. I have also made use of these anthologies to identify clarifying grammatical and spelling revisions made to the originals and to find words that were censored in the original texts, particularly during the Japanese colonial period, and then reinserted by the author or editor for a later anthology.

Paik Jihye, Moon Jiyeon, and Susan Choi have generously given me their permission to translate the essays in this volume.

Work Cited

Glissant, Édouard. *Poetics of Relation*. Translated by Betsy Wing, U of Michigan P, 1997.

Humanism, Empire, and Nation
KOREAN LITERARY AND CULTURAL CRITICISM

PAIK CH'ŎL

Paik Ch'ŏl (1908–85) was born in North Pyongan Province to a small landowning family. He graduated from Sinŭiju Normal School in 1926. He studied abroad in Japan in the English department of the Tokyo Higher Normal School from 1927 to 1931. He joined Nippona Artista Proleta Federacio (the Japanese Federation of Proletarian Artists) in 1930 and began publishing criticism focused on peasant literature. In 1932, he helped to found the Korean Writers' Association. The version of "The Era of Human Description" included here, from 1933, shows his early advocacy of Marxist humanism and proletarian literature, which he later recanted and revised. He spent over a year in prison, from 1934 to 1935, after he was arrested during the second incident of mass arrests of members of Korea Artista Proleta Federacio (the Korean Federation of Proletarian Artists). He published his first pieces of writing expressing political conversion in 1938. He worked for the culture department of the Korea Governor-General's Korean League for National Total Mobilization, writing articles and giving lectures on war literature, propaganda, and Japanese imperial-national literature.

After World War II, Paik was criticized for his activities during the Japanese Empire, but he was also instrumental

in the establishment of the field of literary studies in South
Korea. In 1945, under the request of Im Hwa, he edited two
volumes of the leftist journal *Cultural Front* (문화전선; *Munhwa chŏnsŏn*) then resigned. In the following decades, he was
a professor at Seoul Women's Higher Normal School, Seoul
National University, Dongguk University, and Chungang
University, publishing histories of modern Korean literature
and books on literary criticism. In 1960, he attended the International PEN Club Conference in Brazil and went on to become the Korean representative of that organization, serving
as the head of the international conference held in Seoul in
1971. The first collection of his complete works was published
in 1969. His other major books include *History of New Korean
Literature and Thought* (조선신문학사조사; *Chosŏn sinmunhak sa-
josa*; 1947), *Introduction to Literature* (문학개론; *Munhak kaeron*;
1949), *Rebuilding Literature* (문학의 개조; *Munhak ŭi kaejo*; 1958),
The ABCs of Literature (문학 ABC; *Munhak ABC*; 1958), *Theory
of Korean Literature* (한국문학의 이론; *Han'guk munhak ŭi iron*;
1964), *Twentieth Century Literary Arts* (20세기의 문예; *20segi ŭi
munye*; 1964), *A Literary Autobiography: Truth and Actuality* (문학
자서전—진리와 현실; *Munhak chasŏjŏn—chilli wa hyŏnsil*; 1975),
and *The History of the Development of New Korean Literature*
(한국신문학발달사; *Han'guk sinmunhak paltalsa*; 1975).

The Era of Human Description

The Chosun Ilbo (조선일보; *Chosŏn ilbo*)
29 August–1 September 1933
Colonial Korea

1.

"In a certain sense, all of the central problems of philosophy
can be said to lead us back to the questions of what man is
and what the metaphysical position and status is which he
occupies within the totality of being, world, and God. A set
of older thinkers were not in error in being in the habit of
making the starting point of all philosophical questioning
the 'place of mankind in the universe'—that is, in having
an orientation concerned with the metaphysical site of the
essence of 'man' and his existence."
                        —Max Scheler, "On the Idea of Man"

This is the antiprogressive view belonging to philosophical anthropology, the naive child and idealistic core of
contemporary philosophy that tries to return it to the time
before the Young Hegelians.[1] Scheler's perspective on the
human is in the same vein as the Kantian one, which attempts to make the form of being of the human the foundation for the form of being of all existing things.[2] In the
philosophy of today's humanists—from its latest and most
typical representative, Husserl's phenomenology, to the

interpretive phenomenology (or ontology) of his disciple Heidegger, which represents the philosophical spirit of the contemporary crisis—they offer up interpretations of the human to the effect that "all objects are not themselves beings, but rather rough sketches abstracted from the being Man."

In enumerating this inauspicious statement at the beginning of this essay, I of course do not intend to offer a critique of philosophical anthropology.[3] As we should not understand the human as philosophical anthropology does, as an absolute and eternal being, the concept of the human addressed in this essay is not the human defined in that sense.

The human that I mean here, in relation to literature rather than philosophy, was originally defined philosophically under the presupposition of a mutual determination between the history of nature and the history of the human being; therefore, this human refers to "real, active men, as they are conditioned by a definite development of their productive forces and of the intercourse corresponding to these, up to its furthest forms" (Marx's "The German Ideology"), and is by no means a human that transcends its relations with external beings.[4]

As I am a layperson in philosophy, my regular use of this difficult philosophical statement concerning the human, which here I define through the literary essay, is not something I do naturally, and I wish to advance this essay while refraining from this statement's misuse of the term *human* in its basic meaning and endeavoring as much as possible not to stray from the line of literature.

It is the era of human description in literature . . . (*description* is not a very precise term). In taking up this term to try to explain the literary character of the present, I would point to the fact that in our immediate contemporary moment, the attention and concern of the general writer are concentrated on human description, and at the same time I think that there has never been a time in the present or the past of literature when the concern of the writer has turned away from human description.

(29 August 1933)

2.

We can see why literature until now has always been given to human description if we only understand that literary history represents one of various aspects of history, one part of the history of ideology, and that literature is that which records knowledge of and relationships to human life.

More than anything else, the works of all the great writers of the past prove this truth concretely, but whenever they wrote, the point of greatness of any one of these writers is usually determined by whether they described truthfully the human of their own era.

Historical character types and models are described superbly in their works; not just in Shakespeare's *Hamlet* or Cervantes's *Don Quixote*, but in all the other works of great authors—for example, Dante's *Vita Nuova* (Beatrice), J. W. Goethe's *Faust* (Mephistopheles), Victor Hugo's *Les Misérables* (Jean Valjean and Cosette), Nikolai Gogol's *The Government Inspector* (Khlestakov), Ivan Turgenev's *Fathers and Sons* (Bazarov) and *Virgin Soil* (Nezhdanov, Solomin, Marianna, etc.), Fyodor Dostoevsky's novels, such as *The Brothers Karamazov*—in each case the presence of superb descriptions of the human determine the important status of their works.

That Michelangelo, the representative artist of the Re naissance era in sculpture, not literature, was concerned only with *The Creation of Eve* and *The Creation of Adam* means that these works were not merely natural phenomena of his genius but that their greatest aspect actually lies in their concern for human creation. I am surprised by a kind of ironic truth when I think about the fact that certainly in *Rosane*, who is like a forest that appears human,[5] but also in Gustave Flaubert's *Madame Bovary*, where humans appear like trees and stones on the roadside, the superior quality of the work is not that of detailed Dutch sceneries or pristine and clear Bohemian landscapes, nor of landscapes replete with the grayish colors of Claude Monet or the dark romantic beauty of Henri Rousseau; rather, the superior quality lies in the accurate depiction of the social life of the human during that era: the bourgeois elegance of the balls, the political meetings, the ladies in the parlors, and, more than anything, the depiction of Emma Bovary, "the most complete portrait that exists in the world of novels." Of course, all the superior humans that appear in these works are not vague humans, but humans with periodicity and historicity and, most important, humans that are described tendentiously.[6] Here I am reminded of Minna Kautsky's famous words from women's history, "The genius writers of every period were always tendentious writers," and at the same time recall the very instructive letter that Friedrich Engels sent her:

> I have no objection to tendentious poetry as such. The father of tragedy, Aeschylus, and the father of comedy, Aristophanes, were both markedly tendentious poets, and no less Dante and Cervantes; indeed the finest aspect of Schiller's *Love and Intrigue* is that it represents the first German politically tendentious drama. The modern Russians and Norwegians, who have produced excellent novels, are all tendentious poets.[7]

(30 August 1933)

3.

I do not have any objection to this statement. Because I think that with all due respect the superior works produced to this point, as well as the main characters who appear in them, were always tendentious. Of course, there are cases in which valuable works are not precisely revolutionary or political but nonetheless retain their being tendentious in an intellectual, moral, or other sense. As Alphonse Daudet states, in some cases genius writers "might not be conscious enough about their own era and their own work to know the degree to which the work fulfills its revolutionary mission," but even though the writer may not have been conscious of it, it is certainly correct to say that the work's essence and its human figures were tendentious.

I cannot continue to discuss the fact of tendentiousness at length but must return again to the program of this essay: the celebrated status of every masterwork lies in human description! However, the main thing to be aware of here is that I said I would define the characteristics of the works of the past, but this does not mean that these works always begin and end with human description; we know, of course, even without Walter Pater's indications, that in addition to the human, nature also appears in objects of art.

How many superior scenes describing nature do we find not just in Greece's poetry of nature but also in all the great works of modernity? But at this point, according to my judgment, the topic of nature does not determine the main value of a work, and in the end, I think nature performs the faithful role of greatly enriching the appearance of the main human characters in the work. In this sense, I think there is no contradiction in stating that human description determines the superior status of art, particularly prose art.

Superior descriptions of the human define the status of a work, which is conditioned on the authors of the past, whether consciously or unconsciously, making human description the central task of literature; furthermore, this tendency to emphasize the description of the human becomes more remarkable the closer one gets to the present. We know that in contrast to Greek poets, writers after the Renaissance, and also modern realists, despite being mistakenly labeled as naturalist writers, actually concentrated their total efforts on human description.

I want to emphasize that in the contemporary moment the idea of human description is demanded most acutely in literature and that this idea should be realized completely in today's literature. The primary reason for doing so is to try to define the historical character of contemporary literature in particular as the era of human description!

Of course, the literature that enacts exemplarily the description of the human, that literary task of our era, is tendentious literature and nothing but it. Why? Because in all the eras of the past, and likewise in the present, tendentious literature is that literature that describes the human truthfully. As Stendhal indicated about Italian literature already some hundred years ago, literature of a particular stage that is deprived of the greatness of world thought (e.g., in the present, the literature of capitalism) cannot discover or describe the true human. Therefore, to create a new history in the present, only a proletarian literature that is cultivated by world thought can discover and describe a true human type of the present and future.

(31 August 1933)

4.

It is no coincidence that proletarian literature, which has this historical superiority, is presently focusing its main efforts on human description! Toward proletarian realism! Toward the dialectical materialist creative method! What they were aiming to describe in the recent calls for socialist realism was a vanguard movement created through group action, socialist heroism, and the embodiment of a living and concrete human. A new type of modern human is being created by Maxim Gorky's *Mother*, Fyodor Panfyorov's *Brusski*, Mikhail Sholokhov's *And Quiet Flows the Don*, and so on, as well as by the superb proletarian writers of Germany and Japan. And this human is a special human that cannot be seen in works of the past, a human type that approaches perfection.

However, I know that outside this new literature that represents the literary task of human creation, there exists on the other side a legitimate literature of capitalism that is also currently focusing its concern and attention on the place of human description. In the literature of Marcel Proust and James Joyce, which is the most famous of the literature of capitalism, or the intellectualist literature of Aldous Huxley, or, otherwise, even the general fiction of personal feeling—the literary concern is certainly focused on the human. Of course, these writers do not take the genuine human with all its sides as their object and rather try to analyze the human internally, in parts. In this sense, Benjamin Crémieux's statement that "the period from 1918 until 1930 is the era of the analysis of the human!" can be seen to be confessing the contemporary particularity of every bourgeois literature. These writers are trying to record human psychology through a psychological method of analysis.

We know that even though the literatures of the two classes are not identical, they are both concentrating their main efforts on human description. Human description! The contemporary﹐literary character is focused there, one side having the creative method called socialist realism and the other having the literary method called psychological realism.

(1 September 1933)

Notes by the Editor

1. As noted in the introduction, for this translation I have used the original newspapers articles from *The Chosun Ilbo*, as archived in the *The Chosun Ilbo* online news library; see Paik, "In'gan."

2. This translation is Nabe's (184).

3. I translate 인간학 (*in'ganhak*) as "philosophical anthropology." *In'ganhak* is a translation of the Japanese term 人間学 (*ningengaku*), or "the study of the human," as it appears in the works of Watsuji Testurō and other Japanese philosophers of the time. In contrast to anthropology that is based in ethnographic research, typically translated as 인류학 (*illyuhak*), 인간학 (*in'ganhak*) combines transcendental moral philosophy with the cultural-anthropological study of cultivation and human relations. See "Note on the Translations."

4. This translation is Lough's (36).

5. Paik's reference to a Rosane or Rozanne is unclear. I decided on Rosane, the titular character of Jean Desmarets de Saint-Sorlin's *Rosane, histoire tirée de celles des Romains et des Perses*.

6. See the introduction on tendency, tendentious literature, and the New Tendency Group.

7. Paik leaves out the rest of the paragraph, which would support his argument against an overly formulaic proletarian literature. Engels goes on to state that "tendentiousness should arise out of the plot itself without being explicitly pointed out" (qtd. in Krojzl 303).

Literature for Thirty Million Koreans: What Kind of Literature Do the People Desire?

Literature (문학; *Munhak*)
May 1950
South Korea

After liberation we advocated a new literary movement, and today, six years later, I do not readily have the confidence to say how far our literature has advanced, but the fact is that the reading public has advanced much more than us.[1] This is the case in more than just literature; we understand that when we bring into view the state of advancement of all the artistic movements, we can point out that the public that stands at the periphery of these spheres is in a much more advanced position than the artists who are in direct control of them. As one powerful piece of evidence, I offer the example of a symphony performance this year and the listeners who supported it. As a dilettante, I will offer a dilettantish interpretation: in wandering within or on the edges of various fields of art that departed anew after liberation, or in looking at those fields that deviated from the line of departure and regressed, or even just in the domain of music, the signs are clear that symphonic music has distinguished itself; however, what I noted at this performance, and each of the many times that I have gone to the symphony hall, was the success of the symphony and the listeners' quiet attitude of appreciation, which we did not see in the old days. First of all, to calculate the numbers, in Seoul alone we can estimate the dedicated symphony-going public at more than ten thousand, and this number increases significantly when counting nationwide, a new cultural trend of the public that emerged this year.

Even though vocal music and the symphony are both music, comparatively the symphony belongs to an abstruse field that is difficult for the general public to approach. And when we compare the symphony to fictional literature, which is the representative form of contemporary literature, there is no need to explain that our literature has an incomparably larger popularity. As I have submitted before and do so again here, I have some degree of evidence in hand that in the field of literature as well the reading public is very advanced compared to our writers. First of all, the fact that recently many newcomers have appeared in our literary sphere provides evidence of this. Concerning the fiction of the newcomers, in another essay I have expressed my dissatisfaction that they do not constitute a new generation of writers.

On the other hand, it is a fact the literary techniques that these newcomer writers are attaining, beginning with their sentences, have closed in on the establishment, and if we see these techniques as a matter of the relative age, and so on, of the newcomers, or as something attained in the years since liberation, then we can feel the great speed of their advancement compared to the literary advancement of the establishment. Furthermore, I know firsthand that this quality applies not only to the people who have appeared in the literary sphere. I know that many literary scholars like me who have spoken with university students in the arts and sciences will feel the same way, that there is a truly large number of young university students who are at the same level as the newcomers to the literary sphere—we can estimate hundreds in Seoul alone and assume that it goes over a thousand nationwide. If we go down one class from this level there is the young literary public that adores literature, and if going down another class we count the reading public that reads and understands fiction, it is not a purely imaginary calculation to reason that the size of the reading public that can truly understand fiction is upward of one million. And it is a fact that lately this literature-reading public of one million is actually advancing at a surprising speed compared to the dormant state of the litterateurs who control the literary establishment. This is a fact that can only surprise and frighten our establishment figures, but it must also be a fortuitous and good situation for the future of our literary sphere. The one million readers at the periphery of our literature today stand as testifiers and witnesses to the trends of our literature.

A number of times in our literary history we have intentionally strategized the popularization of literature, but if we ignore the actuality of both university students and the public and unilaterally drag literature into an underground cellar, it can only become mechanical. When the reading public overtakes it and advances, literature has no need to reject popularity and also no means to reject popularity. At that moment not only should literature breathe with the people and walk alongside them, but also if the writer, for their part, takes the posture that they alone are a superior artist and relegates the masses to the world of the herd, then literature will not go beyond narcissistic sentimentalism. And if literature then ignores the character and tendencies of the people's literary desires and isolates itself in narrow personal taste, then it will become an escapist aristocratism, and nowadays there is certainly a sentimental and aristocratic side to our literary sphere. On the other hand, when we think of popular taste only in terms of vulgar things, because it is described and understood vaguely, and when in coveting the most readers possible we push written works into the crude world of sexually desirous and outrageous content, such fiction becomes so-called popular fiction, and this vulgarity is another distorted tendency in our literary sphere.

If the former tendency biases literature and the latter makes literature heretical, our literature must square and overcome each of these two tendencies and construct one genuine literature, and a path toward this construction becomes possible when we neither ignore the public nor interpret it vaguely but rather gauge the specific reading public of the era and reflect and raise into actuality its intellect, tastes, and wishes.

What kind of fiction, then, does the reading public want from our literature under such circumstances? In a word, literature that feels familiar, fiction that is close to people's lives, and works that describe the situations about which the reading public is greatly concerned. The protagonists of Balzac and Dostoevsky were characters that readers could commonly see in their surroundings and about whom they could feel familiarity or hatred. This is not a matter of authors simply contributing to the charting of the everydayness of popular life, but rather this effect becomes possible when these authors select and grasp something representative, typical, or commonplace from the actuality of public life and its surroundings and then elevate it to literary reality. Largely, this task is not a matter of thinking vaguely from democratic principles but rather begins from doing observational research into all the features that form our actuality at the present stage, and if there is confusion or corruption there, we should not only understand it through simple concepts of politics and the standard of living but should grasp its true reality in the actual life of the people, with the indigenous organizations, societal customs, family system, and conventional ethics of this land in the background; then, at the same time as we are able to observe the transforming face of democracy during this transitional period, we can truthfully discover and create typical characters of this actuality—representative good and bad people, old ethics, and new feelings—and these characters and ethics will come to constitute the existence and the thoughts, the real feelings of happiness, sadness, love, and hatred, that the reading public holds directly. If the path of our literature were somewhat more normal in this respect, then these problems might be unexpectedly simple. If writers love and understand the public, and if their literature is not inclined toward the biases of an elevated solitude practiced deliberately for its own sake, then they will not be allowed to lapse into an odd vulgarity. Then a genuine popular literature that today has emerged partially will resolve single-handedly the issue of creating a popular literature that is at the same time a pure literature. Our fiction will not be a private thing belonging to an authorial individual or to some people with like-minded taste, but rather it will go along with and guide the era, becoming a literature and a teacher of the people of three thousand ri. And if in the future sympathy and knowledge develop between our nation and humanity, then when the thirty-eighth parallel has collapsed,[2] the time will come when our fiction is the literature of the whole nation of thirty million, as the editorial board of this journal hoped; and more than that we will be able to imagine our fiction becoming a literature belonging to the whole of world humanity in an ideal era in the distant future. Is this not a leaping pose? The body, or our contemporary spirit, is sitting in reality while its wings are always ready to take off in the direction of the future.

Notes by the Editor

1. For this translation, I referred to the original essay published in *Literature*; see Paik, "Samch'ŏnmanin."

2. By the collapsing of the thirty-eighth parallel, Paik means the reunification of the nation of Korea, presumably by peaceful means.

What Comes after Naturalism: The Unity of the External Human and the Psychological World

Literary Arts (문학예술; *Munhak yesul*)
January 1956
South Korea

What kind of transformative leap does our literary world promise in 1956?[1] What is sure to happen? Or rather, what should we put our willful effort toward making happen?

This year, I think that our literary world must do a variety of critical work to contribute clear literary-historical consciousness to the rebirth of our literary establishment. If we look around at the movements of our literary world, even referencing the works of just the last year, we have conventionalized the outmoded perspectives of the works as is and have done so unconsciously. These works may contain new tendencies in terms of twentieth-century Euro-American fiction, but they are also highly prejudicial; therefore, they are certainly not representative trends that have adapted to our literary-historical position and necessity, and they give the impression of being coincidental. When we look objectively at where the causes lie for our world of writing being put in such a state, we see that this world should actually be criticized for negligence and disregard, as well as for contradiction and impulsiveness.

After liberation, we claimed to champion the establishment of a national literature and pursued that task for ten years, in principle speaking of our concerns about both regional and worldly, both established and contemporary things; however, we actually could not cause reflection on any victories, new tendencies, or new methods concerning the concrete writing practices of literature. This failure is also an indication of the impoverishment of our literary theory and criticism, that it essentially cannot influence literary works. But more than that, the failure causes one to reflect on the total powerlessness of our literary world—first, our literary world lacks a clear historical purpose regarding the nation, and, second, it lacks a vital will to create the nation and instead proves that its genuine literary-historical grasp of the nation is insufficient.

In the end, we return to the problem of literary history. Crafting a national literature today is significant because of the power of the immediate, living, and actual anti-Japanese and anticommunist situation; however, even though we do not lack in such factors, it is not a matter of dealing with them emotionally from the citizen's standpoint but rather a matter of endeavoring to be truly capable of obtaining literary efficacy by transforming all the inspiration and energy directed toward these factors into the ethics and energy required for the practice of writing literary works. In other words, for literature to be hostile toward the Japanese Empire and struggle against it, it is more important that our literary works be of a standard higher than that of the works produced in the Japanese literary world, and that our works compete and win against them, than it is for us to write works that directly lay bare emotions concerning the Japanese Empire; this direction is also essential literarily. Literarily, this also entails the pursuit of an identical efficacy from the standpoint of anticommunism; the national literature that we craft should rise to the level of superior world literature through powerful writing practices and generate its effectiveness only through the directions and actions that make such practices their goal. To do so, we not only grasp the right situation and meaning of literary history, and absorb all these actual and timely problems into literary history, but also seek in our current literature the necessary relationships between our national and regional situation and the literary-historical things of our past, advancing their dutiful course and concrete methods through practice.

First of all, the phenomenon of contradiction through negligence in our current literary world is nothing but the sign of a literary-historical contradiction through habit, and therefore some sort of practical significance and method that overcomes this contradictory phenomenon must be clarified.

In terms of literary history, our literary world has been unable to go beyond the boundaries of naturalist literature. Of course, looking back at the history of our new literature in the thirty years following the founding of the Creation Group in 1919, we can see that there were many movements in our literary history that were opposed to naturalism, and it is not as though there are no examples of writers who individually created lyrical tendencies that were different from the tendencies of naturalism; however, viewed more broadly, these were all temporary and individual phenomena and none of them were successful at wholly overcoming naturalism as a literary trend or method and truly bringing about a transition to something new. After some time, they were all restored again to something naturalist. Even when we think about literary theory, though there are examples of individuals who truly left behind the concept of naturalist literature and thought about a completely new fiction, such movements have never arisen throughout a whole generation. The same can be said about examples of literary works. The personal novel and the novel of custom, which belong to our fiction, were mainstream around 1935, and even today in 1955 they have undoubtedly already become the world and method for the majority of writers. In the end, each time, the topics merely changed; the fact is that the literary spirit and methods of our literary world are still stagnant at the naturalist stage. We need to first apply rigorous reflection to this issue.

However, through some collective steps taken mostly by newer writers in poetry and fiction over the last two or three years, it is a fact that new and powerful tendencies have emerged. This is what I mentioned at first. However, here I would like to point out that if we ask whether the tendencies of these new writers represent the vitality of a whole literary world emerging from some kind of literary-historical resistance, they give the impression that they do not have a literary-historical and authentic status. However, the truth is that the new tendencies that the poets here in our country pick up are those taken from the new twentieth-century tendencies of European literature more than they are determined by an independent standpoint concerning literature. There are two problems. First, I doubt if the new twentieth-century tendencies of European literature can be applied as contemporary tendencies in our literature. Second, I doubt if these new tendencies of present-day European literature, when viewed through literary history in Europe, actually signify its traditions.

Let me begin with the former. That twentieth-century European literature resisted modern literature, and particularly nineteenth-century naturalism, meant a huge and necessary transition in literary-historical terms. However, the problem is what came after this transition. In looking at the many literary trends of the twentieth century, we see that perhaps it was good that they all took a position that opposed and destroyed the nineteenth century, but there was a tendency to stop at opposing the nineteenth century for its own sake and being limited to single tests and experiments that could not become some sort of new literary-historical scene that would be its own tendency. As René Marill Albérès stated, these trends all ended up being just intellectual adventures. For example, one powerful twentieth-century literature among them is so-called psychological literature, and it is necessary for us to first examine its literary-historical significance.

The naturalist literature of the nineteenth century mainly grasped the essence of the human by describing its exterior, but against the notion that that was the extent of the methods of literature, psychological literature conversely sought the interior world of the human and

brought about a huge transition in the world of literature. This was certainly the discovery of a new continent
in literature. It found there a different aspect of the essence of the human. Why? Because the essence of the
human was not only on the exterior but also on the interior and was not only in the rational world but also in
the irrational. On this point we must acknowledge the
literary-historical contributions of pioneering twentieth-
century psychological literature. However, the result
was not complete. That is to say, this literature fell into
a partiality similar to when a person lacking sight holds
one part of a large animal and claims it is the whole animal. Just as the exterior world of the human is not the
whole of the human, its interior also cannot be its whole.
Therefore, the limitless interior world does not satisfy
all the necessary requirements of literary history and is
only whatever a reactive psyche concocts in response to
simple exterior literature. Of course, this kind of excess
of interior consciousness is not a simple fact of psychological coincidence, but behind it there is a temporal and
social background such as the particularity of the social
position of the hapless modern intellectual; therefore, I
was opposed to twentieth-century psychological literature because I thought that the problem of the form of
the contemporary human—the main topic discussed at a
conference of Western European intellectuals that took

place around 1935—was important and groundbreaking for literature as well.[2]

If in literary-historical terms the twentieth century's opposition to nineteenth-century literature did not completely negate or discard it but rather continued it and developed it, then the propensities and one-sided excesses, such as those in psychological literature, would not have emerged. If twentieth-century literature says that nineteenth-century literature limits itself to the naturalist side when grasping the essence of the human, then shouldn't it help that side to thrive in a rational way while pursuing the other side and seeking to replenish it and unify both sides? I think that the topic of the 1935 conference of intellectuals was an opportunity to discuss views of the human and the world of literary works on the psychological side and to criticize the imbalances. Because the significance of political criticism against fascism was strong at that conference, many people ignored the literary-historical criticisms and lessons that arose there, but the conference certainly entailed essential revisions to contemporary literature. What I felt in that year while reading the fiction of interior consciousness from the new writers was, "Aren't they thoughtlessly appropriating this?" I thought that if this literature is not authentic in the West and is just one prejudicial expression, it cannot come to us and become authentic literature; furthermore, when we include problems such as the complexes of our contemporary literature and its high degree of formalism, we need to reflect again on the contrivances of our contemporary poetry and fiction. I have remarked on this issue various times, but when we receive the contemporary tendencies and methods of foreign literature, we should always consider rigorously our actual literary-historical standpoint and the meaning of these foreign literatures for literary-historical development here.

In our present situation, can we expect that something will arise in a literary-historical manner? What are the topics that have been added to our literature in 1956?

One thing that is clear is that naturalist literature—its view of the human and its methods—has become obsolete for us as well. Our writers still unconsciously imitate elements of naturalism through sheer inertia, and even though I think these elements of naturalism are worn out, it is not easy for writers to break this habit, and our literature should endeavor to liquidate it completely. It seems out-of-date to once more call for the liquidation of naturalist literature, but looking honestly at our literary world, I find that this resolution is actually required more than anything else. I feel this concerns more than our literary world. It is also necessary for the advanced twentieth-century literature of Europe and America to return first to the border it shares with naturalism and then to depart again from there. Why? Because when we go searching in the wrong direction, it is correct and effective methodologically for us to return to the point of departure and depart again.

In the history of modern Korean literature, naturalist literature is one of the mainstream literatures of the second generation and an authentic literature representative of that generation's latter half. In our country, naturalist literature's literary-historical position is, in another sense, more important for the thought of new literature. Through the reception of naturalist literature, we came to write the only true short fiction in our modern literature. That is to say, because the ground for our literature was prepared by naturalism, our activity could not begin without making it the base. The worlds and methods of our newcomers' fiction represent a path that is in a sense too new and too out of joint because it is too remote from this naturalist grounding.

What we are now calling a new departure directly from naturalism is not something trite. It will come about through the method of taking as a critical object the process of the advanced European and American literature of the twentieth century, while at the same time anticipating a situation in which we resolve in a unified way the back-and-forth, contradictory relationships that circulate in modernity and the contemporary moment. To make this new departure a true literary-historical overcoming and not a bluff is to aim to enact qualitative progress rapidly concerning such complicated relationships.

What, then, are the methodological tricks for breaking away from and overcoming naturalism? One can offer a number of main recommendations.

First, what kind of humans are the protagonists in recent literature and the characters in recent works? After all, doesn't new literature become a problem of a new human? The essence of this human must be to absorb the psychological literature of the twentieth century, but in relation to the human that the new literature creates, we should ask how much weight to give to interior and psychological matters; this human should at least not be defined by the prejudices and excesses such as those in psychological literature. Viewed from "the form of the contemporary human," this concept of the human is one that establishes balance and harmony between the brain and the four limbs; viewed from the contemporary human's subjectivity, it means a human that unifies subject and object. What I want to say is that it is inauthentic when the psychology of a human in a literary work does not establish in succession the cause and effect of actions. Or at least it is unsound. Literature's search for the essence of the human is not directed toward an individual sufferer with weak nerves, but rather toward a human in the sense of humanity, who represents a great and total method and meaning. Essentially, this kind of human cannot live only as a psyche but can exist only in relation to and in unity with a world of action; thus when we create a human in literature in the future, I believe that first opposing the mechanical human of naturalist literature and then always seeking the world of the psyche in the mind's relation to actual conditions will become central opportunities for literary development.

Second, let us add ethicality to the internal-external relations of this human. Let us say the human does not move mechanically, nor does it act as it pleases. One can view the history of humanity as a history of death and say that one sees eras and actualities as hospital rooms, but this would be a prejudice and therefore not an authentic opinion. One can view this human not as rational and reasonable but as irrational, contradictory, and incomprehensible, but that is surely not a correct opinion. Indeed, the twentieth century is a dark environment and hardly a situation in which to make normal plans. However, that view expresses a sort of contemporaneity rather than historicity. If it is difficult to have a clear historical perspective here, we must at least be able to trust in humanistic historicity and the essence of the human.

We know the example of a drunken person who, even in the middle of the night, takes various wrong paths but finally finds their house, and we can trust that this approach is natural. There is an important historical significance now in criticizing ethically all the unhealthy phenomena of the present moment and in guiding one's life view and worldview stoically, out of a faith that the direction of human history points toward a happy world.

Third, it is evident that when we seek a literary method that corresponds to the meaning of the human that we are aiming at, we know this method has a three-dimensional and synthetic essence compared to the previous methods of naturalism, which are superficial and personally descriptive. Adding to this the three-dimensionality of contemporary mechanical civilization, and the pleasure and visibility of its beauty and speed, and furthermore, if we combine them with the methods and reality of contemporary art (e.g., film and television), then the method that we seek is not simply an abstract theory, and we can discover and reinforce an unexpectedly new and powerful method of creation that emerges from writing practice.

Fourth, in relation to the problem of human creativity and method, we must put into practice the search for classical literature and its traditions for the sake of this new craft of literature. If we ask about overcoming naturalism or where to locate the task of guiding the independent character and methods of prose literature, we are premising the question on the inheritance of classical literature. Therefore, I think that this year it is necessary for our literature to have a more organic and practical relationship with the researchers of classical literature and that after we form that relationship it will be necessary to expend all our effort to enliven it and develop it into an actual method.

Notes by the Editor

1. A revised version of this essay by Paik, under the title "Toward the Overcoming of Naturalism: Through a Love of Tradition and the Human" ("자연주의의 극복을 위하여—전통과 인간에 쏟아지는 애정으로"; "Chayŏnjuŭi ŭi kŭkpok ŭl wihayŏ—chŏnt'ong kwa in'gan e ssodajinŭn aejŏng ŭro") appears in Paik, *Paik Ch'ŏl p'yŏngnon sŏnjip.* I translated the original 1956 text that appears in *Literary Arts*; see Paik, "Chayŏnjuŭi twi e."

2. Paik is referring to the International Congress for the Defense of Culture, held in Paris in 1935. See note 2 in the introduction.

Sŏ Insik

Sŏ Insik (1905–unknown) was a socialist activist and intellectual of the Japanese colonial period. He was born in Hamhŭng in South Hamgyong Province. In 1924, he graduated from the Chungang Normal School in Seoul and then went to Tokyo, entering the philosophy department of Waseda University. In 1928, while active in the eastern cell of the Korean Communist Party in Japan, he was promoted to head of the Totsuka cell of the Korean Communist Youth Association. He organized for the association within the New Scientific Research Association, a socialist research group begun by exchange students in Tokyo. He became a member of the anti-Japanese umbrella organization Sin'ganhoe and was subsequently expelled from Waseda University.

In 1929, Sŏ went to China and discussed the best course for rebuilding the Korean Communist Party with the Marxist-Leninist Group. He returned to Korea at the end of 1930. In February 1931, he became a leader and scribe for the propaganda division of the League to Reestablish the Korean Communist Party but decided to dissolve that organization at the Yŏngdŭngp'o Conference two months later. He distributed manifestos on topics such as the internal problems of the Sin'ganhoe, labor unions, and textile worker strikes.

He helped form the Korean Communist Association in Taegu later that year and was tasked with publishing its journals, *Beacon* (봉화; *Ponghwa*) and *Communist* (코뮤니스트; *K'omyunisŭt'ŭ*). The Japanese police arrested him the following year. On 21 April 1933, at the Taegu regional court, he was sentenced to five years in prison for violating publishing laws and the Peace Preservation Law.

Only after serving his prison sentence did Sŏ begin publishing the kind of erudite philosophical articles on culture and literature found here. From 1939 until the end of World War II, in many newspaper and journal articles, he developed arguably colonial Korea's most philosophically sophisticated discussions of dialectics, labor, nation, state, culture, literature, modernity, and the East Asian Community. The essays translated and collected here show his range as a thinker, addressing issues as diverse as the philosophical foundations of East Asian culture, nostalgia, and literary realism. At the end of the war, he went to North Korea with the dream of actualizing a new socialist society. He died sometime in the 1950s, and his death may have been at the hands of Kim Il Sung and the elites in the Korean Workers' Party, who were drawn mainly from the anti-Japanese guerrilla movement in 1930s Manchuria and solidified power by purging the Soviet and Yan'an factions.

The Idea and Form of Eastern Culture: Its Particularity and Generality

The Dong-a Ilbo (동아일보; *Tonga ilbo*)
3–12 January 1940
Colonial Korea

1.

When we discuss Eastern culture, we usually think about the culture of China as the standard and then think of India and Japan second.[1] And when we discuss Eastern culture, it is also customary for us to mean something opposed in essence to Western culture. However, it appears that various scholars, including an authority in sinology, Tsuda Sōkichi, have agreed that we cannot refer to Eastern culture in the same way that we lump together the cultures of various European countries and call them Western culture.

Since before the modern era, the various peoples of Europe formed one unified cultural sphere called world culture and lived that way; however, until their arrival in the modern era, the various peoples of the East formed independent cultural spheres, each living in isolation without deep internal connections in terms of cultural history. In Europe, already in the Roman era the classical culture of Greece and eastern Christian thought unified into one and established a single cultural and ideological substance. The world was one to these Europeans because their cultures expanded as they passed through the medieval Christian world and thrived within a single culture until arriving at the scientific world of modernity.

One can see the cultures of all these peoples as the many branches of a large stem river that originated on Mount Olympus in Greece and has split into many off-shoots. Therefore, Western culture is not a contentless figure of speech and indicates a single cultural substance that has a fixed volume, solidity, and color.

However, in the East the situation is different. Indian culture originated in the Ganges River basin and Chinese culture was born in the Yellow River basin. The towering mountain peaks in the southeast of the continent obstructed cultural exchange between the two nations. China's importation of Buddhism from India during the Han Dynasty probably has the most significance in terms of cultural exchange between the two nations. However, even imported Buddhism could not bring about some kind of fundamental transformation in China's native traditional thought and, on the contrary, underwent a transformation suitable to the native culture of this hard-headed nation and was completely absorbed. It is absolutely clear that China has not contributed any cultural achievements to India.

These two pillars of culture had neither the same place of origin nor the same basin where they could join, as with the cultures of the various nations of Europe. The two nations breathed in separate worlds culturally. Therefore, there can be European cultural history in Europe, but in the East, there cannot be Eastern cultural history in a strict sense. There are Indian cultural history and Chinese cultural history.

(3 January 1940)

Therefore, the term *Eastern culture* is in fact a contentless figure of speech or, if not, still not more than a recent myth. However, the fact that Eastern culture did not establish a single substance does not necessarily mean that the term has not had any worthwhile meaning.

Eastern culture is the culture produced by the various nations of the East, and its content does not necessarily differ between each of these nations. However, the many parts that are included within it have a certain distinct particularity unconnected to Western culture. Now, if we speak broadly about each particularity that Eastern culture has that differentiates it from Western things, and if we call these the "Eastern" particularities, then that which has these Eastern particularities can also be called Eastern culture in terms of content.

In this sense, even though *Eastern culture* does not refer to a single substance, can't we use it to refer to the particularity of Eastern culture? And we should not fail to state at the outset that when we use the term *Eastern culture* in this sense, the cultural-historical realities of the various nations of the East that I have mentioned thus far have already provided one formal particularity to Eastern culture.

In the past, G. W. F. Hegel viewed world history as the development of world spirit. Even so, he viewed world history as something established according to the supersession of national spirits.[2] There was only one reason for this. It was because national spirit that had world-historical significance was nothing other than world spirit. Although this kind of interpretation of history can be posited confidently in the cultural history of Europe, which formed a single world after classical Greece and was developed by various powerful nations taking charge of this world one after another and supplanting one another, this interpretation cannot be applied in the same way to the cultural history of the East, in which China, India, and Japan were all independent of one another and established their own cultures. If you seek at the foundation of Western culture a single internal connection whose warp and woof are the Greek spirit and the Christian spirit, you will find it, but from the outset there was no such world spirit in the cultural history of the East.

National particularity is not clear in Western culture as it is in Eastern culture; on the other hand, particularity of era is not defined in Eastern culture as it is in Western culture. If Western culture is a history of the supplanting of one nation by another, Eastern culture can be viewed as a history of nations standing separately.

2.

However, when we discuss the particularity of Eastern culture, it has become a kind of custom of the contemporary moment for someone to discuss the distinction between Eastern and Western cultures from a metaphysical standpoint. Many thinkers and scholars have actually discussed the difference between Eastern and Western cultures from this standpoint. One can come up with one or two among Westerners, as well, but let us turn to the opinion of Nishida Kitarō!

Nishida, in "The Cultural Circumstances of Classical East and West Viewed from a Metaphysical Standpoint," distinguishes Eastern and Western culture by means of thinking about the problem of existence. Whereas

Western culture views Being as the foundation for existence, Eastern culture sees Nothing as its foundation. He writes,

> Greek culture, which is the origin of Western culture, made the thought of "Being" its basis, and could be called a culture of "Being." Of course, Dionysian culture made a huge contribution to Greek culture. We could say that the Greek nation was originally pessimistic like Indians are. However, the center of Greek culture was Apollonian culture. In Greek philosophy, they thought of tangible and limited things as existence. Form was considered existence. As the etymology of Plato's "Idea" indicates, it was thought to have a formal significance. In Greek philosophy, there was absolutely no thought to view something unlimited or something that exceeded actuality as authentic existence.

As he further notes, however, "Christian culture, which along with Greek culture was an origin of Western culture, is naturally very different from Greek culture. Jehovah is the absolute who transcends this world. He is the creator of this world. He is the ruler of this world. He is the commander of this world." Therefore, "What Christianity contributed to Western culture is the concept of personhood. . . . In medieval philosophy, existence is not ideational, but personal. God is an absolute person. . . . The personhood of God, which is absolutely limitless, is something that transcends our knowledge absolutely." In this sense, "If we say that Greek philosophy is the thought of Being, then we can say that medieval philosophy had significance already as the thought of Nothing. . . . However, the person is not nothing. The person must be the most limited thing. Or he must be someone who limits himself self-destructively. He must be someone who has free will."

(4 January 1940)

In this way, Nishida speaks of Being in the sense that "nature" and "God," the existences conceived by the two sources of Western culture (Greek culture and Christian culture, respectively), are tangible and limited things that are analogous to the organon of production and the personhood of the human.

However, this is not the case for the two pillars of Eastern culture, Indian culture and Chinese culture. "One can say that in contrast to Greece and Christianity, Indian religion was grounded in the deepest thought of Nothing. The gods of Brahmanism are gods that transcend and contain the things of the world and at the same time are everywhere immanent. According to the language of the Upanishads, the gods in this world are wrapped up in a great god as though in a cloth. There is only one being, which does not move but is faster than the mind. None of our senses can perceive it. Even while it moves it does not move. Even while it is far it is near.

It sees the whole world, and whoever sees it in the world cannot disdain it."

This singular being is akin to neither the highest Platonic Idea nor the person-like God of Israel. "Hinduism negates even the person. I consider it unreasonable to think of Hinduism as simply a pantheistic religion. Not only are all things not God in Hinduism, but it even negates all things. This would have to entail an absolute negation or an absolute affirmation. It is similar to the thought that 'form is emptiness' and 'emptiness is form' in Mahayana Buddhism." And

one can view the Way as discussed in the teachings of Laozi and Zhuangzi, who are considered one origin of Chinese culture, to be the thought of Nothing. Laozi said, "The way that can be spoken of / Is not the constant way; / The name that can be named / Is not the constant name. / The nameless was the beginning of heaven and earth / The named was the mother of the myriad creatures."[3] This thought not only negates the beliefs of the Israelites but also negates the wisdom of the Greeks. . . .

Having returned to nature, the teachings of Laozi and Zhuangzi deny that right and wrong, and good and evil, are different within human society. In the Confucian code of ethics, there is no such thought of nature, but only thought of heaven. Confucius states in *The Analects*, "I am thinking of giving up speech. . . . What does [h]eaven ever say? Yet there are the four seasons going round and there are the hundred things coming into being. What does [h]eaven ever say?"[4] Referring to *The Book of Poetry* at the end of *The Doctrine of the Mean*, Zisi quotes the Master, "It is said in another ode, 'His [v]irtue is light as a hair.' Still, a hair will admit of comparison *as to its size*. 'The doings of the Supreme Heaven have neither sound nor smell.'—That is perfect virtue."[5] At the foundation of Chinese culture are the ideas of heaven, the Way, or nature. . . . Meaning that the movement of the sun, the moon, and the stars is the root of all creation and the origin of the human realm. The heavenly realm and the human realm are one. That is, the reason of nature is considered the foundation for social action. . . . The thought of Nothing in Hinduism was intellectual. As thought, it was the negation that negates thought. However, the thought of Nothing in Chinese culture was actional. We could say that as action, it was the negation that negates action.

Then Nishida refers to the Brahma of Hinduism, the emptiness of Buddhism, the nature of Taoism, and the Heaven of Confucianism as Nothing, in the sense that they are all absolutely formless and absolutely cannot be limited.

Following Nishida's point of view, Western culture can be contemplated objectively and disinterestedly, and in opposition to it, the existence conceived in Eastern culture can only be intuited actively and subjectively. In other words, the former can be understood through logic, whereas the latter can only be learned through experience. If there are various types in logic, then the latter cannot be judged according to the logic of Being and can rather be understood only through the logic of Nothing and the logic of action.

Following this line of thinking of Nishida's, Kōyama Iwao, in "The Philosophy of Nothing and the Life behind

It," calls Western culture an objective culture and Eastern culture a subjective culture, in the sense that the specificity of Western culture lies in its objective aspects and the specificity of Eastern culture lies in its subjective aspects. He writes,

> Metaphysical contemplation arises when we ask what kind of relationship substance and phenomena have; when we consider ways of practice, such as religion and morality; and when we ask how to arrive at the world of substance from the world of phenomena.
>
> In relation to the fixing of human attitudes concerning this most fundamental problem, I think there are already two types of attitude. One attitude puts the authentic existence of eternity in front of the human and sets the objective aim that human effort must be directed toward it, and the other attitude puts the authentic existence of eternity behind the human and establishes a subjective home from which the whole effort of the human must depart and to which it must return.
>
> I think that Western culture proceeds in the direction of the former and demonstrates the essence of existence and that Eastern culture proceeds in the direction of the latter and exalts the purification of existence. It is in this sense that the former is an objective culture and the latter is a subjective culture.

To put succinctly what Kōyama is saying, in the West's metaphysics of Being, existence is viewed as something that transcends objectively, and in the East's metaphysics of Nothing, existence is viewed as something that transcends subjectively; therefore, in Eastern culture, the human comes to intervene between objects and existence, whereas in Western culture, phenomena intervene between existence and the human.

3.

If attitudes toward existence in Eastern and Western metaphysics are different in this way, then we should be able to discover various differences between Eastern and Western culture. Why? Because a people's way of talking and thinking about existence will definitively determine the ideas and foundation of that people's culture.[6]

First of all, it is clear that if Western culture, generally speaking, has had an intellectual character, then Eastern culture has had an actional character. If the ultimate ideas of culture are behind the human, in order to reunite with them we must negate the opposition between subject and object, return to the world of action that precedes the subject-object division, and try to learn these ideas through experience. The epistemological subject is initially established as something opposed to an epistemological object. And the epistemological object, as the term *object* suggests,[7] is positioned in front of us. The act of thinking proceeds toward an object that is in front of us. The eye cannot see the eye and the ears cannot hear the ears. Therefore, to see the eyes that see or to hear the ears that hear, the eyes and ears must become things that we observe. The human can only arrive at a substance that is behind itself by appealing to practical experience.

(5 January 1940)

In this situation we could of course contrive an extensive speculation to articulate this substance logically, as we see in Indian philosophy. However, the "Brahman" and the "self" in the phrase "the self becomes one with the Brahman" in Indian philosophy are neither nature nor person but rather absolute Nothing, which transcends all those things. They are the form of the formless and the voice of the voiceless. Therefore, no matter how much we make use of extensive speculation, the form that articulates this substance logically is in the end only a negation.

Atman[8] can only be expressed as *neti neti*[9] (not this, not that). The thought of emptiness in Buddhism, which originated from the same Indian spirit, and of course, the concept of the nameless in Taoism (e.g. "the nameless was the beginning of heaven and earth") are negative expressions of substance that absolutely cannot be expressed.

To say that the articulation of substance is possible only in its negative form means, to put it another way, that the existence of truth can first be grasped only by discarding objective knowledge. To say that something can be articulated only negatively means that the objectification of substance is impossible. If all knowledge is related to an object, the knowledge of truth could only be a knowledge of negation or a knowledge of silence. If knowledge that negates the knowledge of an object is called nirvana, then this is something that can be achieved not by endlessly progressing toward human knowledge, but, conversely, only by endlessly negating and regressing toward the rear.

If so, then what is the knowledge that one can attain by endlessly negating and regressing behind human knowledge? This knowledge is only the wisdom of nirvana realized through personal practice (asceticism).

However, ideas (Idea) or God in Western culture (here I ignore the modern culture of the West and discuss only the cultures of antiquity and the Middle Ages—see below) can be grasped as some kind of form through contemplation, because they transcend us as something natural or person-like. The Brahman and self, or emptiness and nature, of the East can only be learned through experience, but Idea and God in the West can be understood (or at least we can try to understand them). The learning and arts of the West that flowered brilliantly after Greece crystallize the spiritual vitality of all the nations of broader Europe with the purpose of defining Idea and God.

In the West, science and logic developed, whereas in the East teaching and training developed. In the East, learning that did not require a path to enlightenment, as in Hinduism or Buddhism, or proper conduct, as in Confucianism, was not viewed as learning, but in the West, from the era of ancient Greece, there developed learning for learning's sake and art for art's sake. As opposed to the East, where personal practice and asceticism were essential, in the West observation and analysis were required. Isn't this the reason that in the East there is wisdom and in the West knowledge, and wise men are received better than philosophers in the East, but there are many scientists in addition to wise men in the West?

(6 January 1940)

Any action, then, belongs to an individual practical subject, and knowledge belongs to a universal epistemological subject.[10] Action adheres to the life of the human and cannot shed its subjective and particular quality; knowledge leaves behind its human responsiveness and aims at objectivity and universality. The content and fruits of action have a kind of dialogic and grammatical character and require familiarity and secrecy, whereas the content and fruits of knowledge have a monologic and logical character and demand the approval of everyone.

Therefore, more than anything, we must see that Western culture is completely independent from the productive subject of practice, has objective universality, and can reign over the collective assets of the entirety of humanity, whereas Eastern culture cannot shed its responsiveness to the productive subject of practice and has a more or less subjective and esoteric quality. Western culture can be learned by any national people if only they possess the corresponding intellectual cultivation, but the spirit of Eastern culture arrives at the absurd conclusion that it is difficult to become enlightened if one is not well-acquainted with an expert and master who has achieved enlightenment concerning the strange meaning of all the paths of nature. In the East, there have been masters, beginning prominently with the Buddha and Confucius and continuing more modestly with the sword masters and weavers, who have found one by one various secret methods for following these paths and have attained a state of free will. In the East, the truth is never something ascertained and is rather learned through experience. In a sense, maybe all the cultured men of the ancient East were indeed cultivated men who took this path.

And if, first, Western culture is the production of knowledge and Eastern culture is a form of action, then can't we say, second, that Western culture had a compositional and systemic quality, whereas Eastern culture had an intuitive and fragmented quality? Knowledge is organized and systemic, but action is intuitive and formal. The whole of that which is composed can be divided into parts. Collecting the parts and making a whole is called composition.

However, that which is formal certainly cannot be divided as a whole. We call form the transformation of one whole into another whole. If a machine is an example of a transformation of something organized, life is an example of a transformation of something formal.

The function of knowledge is of course to analyze things and synthesize them. The function of the intellect is to divide intuited material according to various abstract requirements and then to synthesize and elevate that material by way of a mediatory whole. Therefore, if Western culture is the product of intellectual composition, we can dismantle and synthesize again any given philosophy or science, or even the internal connections between various fields of an era's culture, through a fixed logical operation. And if Western culture, viewed from the continuities in its development, followed, to a degree, a regulated and orderly process of division and unifica-

tion and developed from something abstract and particular into something concrete and general, then maybe
we can even trace these internal, necessary connections
through a fixed logical operation.

However, if Eastern culture is, as the theorists say, a
product of simple acting intuition, then maybe we can
discover a kind of metamorphosis that moves toward the
whole within Eastern culture, but I fear that imputing
analysis and synthesis, and division and unification, to
Eastern culture would instead lead to misunderstanding
the essence of culture. The majority of Eastern learning
is essays or a record of words and deeds. It is only a se-
quence from one intuition to another intuition, without
the mediation of logic. Actually, it is not the sequencing of
intuition and intuition, but only each intuition expressed
fragmentarily, severed from the others.

(7 January 1940)

Perhaps in such a situation it is not possible to discover
metamorphosis in the strict sense, but only to record
plainly the everyday truths experienced by this or that
scholar at this or that time. A formless truth hides here
and there and appears here and there. The existence of
eternity congeals within a single moment's intuition.

The way of congealing differs according to place and time. "Short speech, few words" and "one stroke, one touch" come to imply the mysteries of heaven and the human realm. If so, then Zen Buddhism, which advocates revelation without dependence on literature,[11] might be the pinnacle of Eastern learning. If the truth is that there is no need for a pure experience of everything or for endless discussion, and that one can achieve enlightenment suddenly with a single thunderous shout, then learning seems useless in the first place. Many sects of Buddhism, in trying to express theoretically this formless truth instead fabricated strange constructs and pedantic logic. In Hinduism, it is the same. However, it is not possible for strange constructs and pedantic logic to express the formless in tangible form.

One might say that even if Indian philosophy is speculative in this way, it has organization and systematicity. However, Eastern learning is learning that cultivates a life attitude of receiving truths more than of cultivating the thing of truth itself. As stated, the particularity of Eastern culture lies in making its goal practical self-improvement.

Anyway, if the essence of Eastern learning lies in the plain expression of fragmented intuitions, then it is certain that we cannot find division and development in Eastern learning as we can in Western learning. Until later generations, philosophy in India belonged to religion, and in China it belonged to politics. It is a preposterous task to search for any separation or independence between learning and other fields of culture, much less any division between the various sciences internal to learning.

I stated before that Western culture is an intellectual composition and that Eastern culture is a product of acting intuition. I stated that the former is intellectual and that the latter is actional. If so, is all knowledge in the East negated, whereas all action is affirmed? In other words, in the East, did human knowledge get negated and regress to the rear, while only the action of the human was affirmed and came to the fore?

If the negation of all objective knowledge appeared as the affirmation of all objective action, then the East would have transformed into a world of beasts. However, the negation of all knowledge does not result in the affirmation of all action. Just the opposite. In Eastern culture, at the same time as all human knowledge was negated, all human action was negated. This is because rather than the East transforming into a wild world of beasts, it transformed into a world of silent sages.

The real intention in negating knowledge in the turn toward existence lay in the fact that humanist knowledge, which obsessed over the object, obscured the true image of existence.

Existence is absolute transcendence and, as an absolute other, is nothingness and emptiness. Not only that, but because human knowledge in its essence is obsessed with the object, it had to be negated. To arrive at existence, all human desires would have to be denied. Or rather, in trying to deny all human desires, all human knowledge, which is obsessed with the object, was negated. Existence is, from the outset, nothingness, emptiness, nirvana, one. Not only that, but that which phenomenalizes existence into being, color, suffering, and the manifold is the human's epistemological subjectivity (i.e., knowledge) and production of meaning. The world of phenomena that presents itself in front of the human appears as suffering (in Buddhism) and anxiety (according to Laozi) because an unenlightened and fixated human shuts out the light of existence that shines out from behind them. In other words, the suffering and anxiety of this world are just the shadow that the human makes standing in front of existence. Therefore, only when we annihilate ourselves completely and achieve a state of selflessness and idleness can we return to the transcendental absolute. And only when we return to the absolute can anguish become Buddha and idleness become free will. Endlessly negating and pushing to the background knowledge directed

toward an object is actually endlessly negating and pushing to the background the will directed toward an object.
And the place where we arrive at the limit of this negation is a nirvana of annihilation and a field of calm futility that have completely extinguished the rich life of the
human (of course, there are objections to seeing Taoist
thought as an asceticism like Buddhism; however, it is
not possible to address them in this summary).

We can see here, then, that action in Eastern culture
is neither action mediated by an object or Being nor an
objective practice, but actually action related to medita-
tion and introspection for the sake of being absorbed
into a state of nondifferentiation and idleness. Action in
the true sense of the term occurs through the interac-
tion between the subject and object of practice. Therefore, just as understanding is established dependent
on the opposition between the subject and object of
knowledge, practice is established dependent on the
opposition between the subject and object of practice.
While understanding, as the unity of the subject and
object of knowledge, and practice, as the unity of the
subject and object of practice, are opposed to each
other, human cultural history forms and progresses
through their respective changes. In a word, we say that
Western culture is intellectual and Eastern culture is actional, but we should not forget that the former, which is

intellectual, has a practical character in a superior sense, and the latter, which is actional, actually has an introspective character.

If in negating the knowledge and conduct of the human, Eastern culture annihilates the rich content of human life and relegates it to selflessness and idleness, this is in contrast to Western culture's affirming and bringing to the fore knowledge and conduct that are directed toward an object and that thereby promote a rich human life. We must advance with a given existence in the foreground. Existence is higher and deeper than phenomena. Plato's highest Idea is the good. The God of Christianity is an absolutely complete person. Therefore, the human effort to attain such existence must elevate and deepen reason and sentiment.

(8 January 1940)

These are ideas that can be attained not by annihilating humanness, but rather by promoting it. In this sense, we can see that Eastern culture is a culture of human alienation and that Western culture is a human-centered culture. Of course, in Western culture as well, clear human-centeredness began with the arrival of modernity. And the culture of the Middle Ages should be viewed as a God-centered culture when compared to modern culture in the history of the West. However, this means that we can make such a comparison only when we place Western culture by itself and observe the eras of its history. When comparing Western culture broadly with Eastern culture, we find that ancient Greek culture, certainly, but also medieval culture were cultures that centered the human.

Of course, we can discover in Eastern thought ideas of the ego that are similar to the concept of the ego that constituted the basis of the modern culture of the West. The atman of Hinduism is one such idea. However, this is neither an individual human ego similar to our own nor a reasonable, logical subject of knowledge. This is an unthinking subject of practice who transcends us downward and forms our background. Just as the eye cannot see the eye and the ear cannot hear the ear, we cannot understand the atman that is our practical subjectivity. This suggests that the atman has neither natural flesh nor spiritual personhood. In this sense, it is truly an absolute other that has no kind of human particularity.

Even within Eastern thought, it seems that the established general opinion is that only Confucianism is a way of thinking that does not eliminate the human. Confucianism is by no means thought that negates the human. However, Confucianism is also thought that centers heaven and not the human. Following Confucius and Mencius, the concept of heaven shed its primitive and mythical character and was purified rationally, germinating the idea of an identity between the heavenly mandate and human life ("What is ordained by heaven is our nature"). And following neo-Confucianism, this thought developed into the principles of heaven and mind. However, the theory of identity between heavenly reason and human life also did not humanize heaven and was not the anthropomorphism of heaven; it heavenized the human and was the theomorphism of people. On this point, Confucian culture, which centered a heaven with neither personhood nor will, also could not, after all, shed the general specificity of Eastern culture, which is to dehumanize the human.

In connection with the proposition that Western culture is a human-centered culture and Eastern culture is a culture of alienation, one thing to pay attention to is the fact that if Western culture generally had an expressive quality, Eastern culture more or less could not shed its symbolic quality.[12] If expression welcomes what is immanent to the human, a symbol suggests something that transcends the human.

An objective transcendent, no matter how much it transcends, can always be made immanent to the human. We can translate as our own immanent essence the fact that the human is tangible and can be limited, no matter how much it is hidden behind phenomena.

(10 January 1940)

More strictly speaking, whatever is not immanent to the human cannot become an object to us in the first place. An objective transcendent is actually nothing but the human making external what is immanent. Between the Idea of the Greeks and the God of Christianity, one was conceived by taking the body of the human as a model, and the other was conceived by taking the personhood of the human as a model. The Idea of Plato and the God of Augustine, while they transcended the human, were actually both expressions of the human itself, in the sense that the human created them.

If there were no beautiful eros concerning a perfect reason that could quietly contemplate, along with eternity, everything in the universe that is created and extinguished with time, then the Greek people could not have conceived of the Idea, and if there were no solemn agape concerning the absolute free will that established the basis for the human's person-like emotions, then

Christians would not have worshipped a person-like God. The Idea that the Greeks loved and the God that the Christians worshipped were actually conceptualized when the human tried to practice its own perfected reason and when it tried to express an unlimited freedom of will. In that sense, both the Idea and God are expressions of humanness. The images of gods that appear in Greek sculptures were themselves expressions of the most perfect body of the human, and the Gothic style of architecture from the Christian Middle Ages was an expression of the longing of the will of humans, who suffer from being bound to the earth, to try to fly toward the limitless heavens.

However, the substance that transcends not above the human, but rather below it, is simply an absolute other. This substance is deeper than Greek nature and deeper than Christian personhood; it transcends even nature and personhood. Eastern existence is this absolute Nothing or absolute emptiness. Therefore, whatever it might have that is human, this cannot appear. The absolute other that transcends below the human, even as it carries something that is immanent to the human, cannot be expressed, because a transcendent that is behind the human cannot be made immanent to the human. That which cannot become immanent to the human cannot be translated as carrying a human essence. When taking the immanentist standpoint that all things belonging to the universe can, to the last, be made immanent to the human, we see "everything that is (Being)" as an externalization of the human. However, not even the human's spirit of omnipotence can translate "what is not (or Nothing)" through its reason, will, and emotions.

As I stated above, if this kind of absolute other, or absolute transcendent, were to be expressed with logic, it could only be articulated negatively, and if it were to be expressed with sensibility, then it could only be suggested symbolically. I say this is why the art of the West is generally intuitive, whereas the art of the East is symbolic. This particularity of Eastern art appears especially conspicuously in Indian art.

The Indian nation traditionally says that giving intuitable shape to the gods is an insult to the gods, and the nation seems to have avoided doing so. Expressing gods in an intuitable and sculptured appearance could be considered a result of exchanges with Greek culture in the western part of India in later generations. In the art of native India, gods were symbolized simply by a dot or a line. However, because the plastic arts construct intuited forms, the Indian nation could not simply remain with such a form in the long term.

(11 January 1940)

When this kind of symbol attains expression, gods are purposefully expressed as inhuman appearances. The strange form that we see in the divine images of India is a product of a spirit that is trying to assign form to what is formless. What makes an appearance of a god manifest symbolically is neither bodily, natural power nor spiritual, mystical power but a nonhuman psychometric power that has completely left behind humanness. The insipid impression left by Indian art, that it is not something of this world, comes from this kind of nonhuman mystique. In this respect, when the scriptures of Mahayana Buddhism express the mysterious power of the Buddha and the endlessly magnificent world of the Buddha, they use unreservedly grandiose numbers that strain our imagination and unbearable overlapping phrases, and such unlimited mode of expression—a peculiar mode that emerges in the attempt to express what cannot be expressed—and unlimited power of the imagination are also a type of symbolic method that comes from the mysticism and the principle of nonpersonhood in the Indian spirit.

To summarize the above, I conclude that Eastern culture is a nonhuman and nonintellectual culture. Of course, following Nishida's explanation, we have seen that the thought of Nothing is at the foundation of Eastern culture, and furthermore, referencing Kōyama's perspective, I have simply tried to state in my own way the specificity of two diametrically different cultures. Therefore, what I have said thus far is an argument that serves a singular hypothesis. Along with the suppositions stated previously, if I may now offer a summary result, the doubt that emerges next is whether a culture that eliminates humanness and negates thought can be seen as a culture in the superior meaning of the term.

Culture is an expression of humanness and a product of knowledge. At least the common notion of culture has been that way thus far. Nothing can be said to the claim that this is one Western notion concerning culture and that it should not be applied in evaluating Eastern culture. However, until a new common notion emerges, one can only use notions that already exist. I will say it again, culture is the expression of humanness and a product of knowledge. Culture is the expression of all the life values that only the human can have, and it can therefore have an objective and universal meaning.

On the other hand, exalting the purity of Eastern culture, the particular cultural spirit of the East, which impoverishes the promotion of humanness and impedes the development of knowledge, causes the exhaustion of the purity of Eastern culture as culture. In other words, this exaltation is a curse for culture. Even if we think that the spirit of Eastern culture can exist only in this place, or that something represents some particular aspect of Eastern culture, such features are neither honorable nor praiseworthy.

It is a fact that on one side of Eastern culture is the particularity of negating humanness and eliminating knowledge. However, that is nothing more than the particularity of Eastern culture. In other words, this particularity originates in opposing Eastern culture to Western culture and having to extract only the particular aspects that are different in nature from it. Therefore, we must understand that these particularities are certainly not Eastern culture. If there is Eastern specificity in Eastern culture, then there must be generality as culture as well. It is likely that the particularity that is Eastern culture can be established because the generality that is culture also exists in Eastern culture. It is a rule that when there is no generality there is also no particularity. When we earlier enumerated the particular aspects of both cultures, we deliberately brought to the surface the commonalities they have as cultures.

However, the particularity of culture is connected to its generality, and when this generality is not delineated, the reason that a particularity is a particularity is not apparent. If so, from now on we must try to delineate the general aspects (those shared with the West) of Eastern culture as culture. And as the connection between generality and particularity is clarified, Eastern culture's particular position in the general cultural-historical course of humanity must be determined. But space is limited, and I will stop this tiresome discussion for now and let's deal with the problems that remain at the next opportunity!

(12 January 1940)

Notes by the Editor

1. For the translation of this essay, I referred to the original articles that appeared in *The Dong-a Ilbo*; see Sŏ, "Tongyang." For all of Sŏ's essays in this volume, I also consulted their reproductions in Sŏ, *Sinmun*. Following Sŏ's inclusion of numbered section breaks in the middle of the newspaper articles, this translation both retains these numbered section breaks and divides the essay into its original daily installments.

2. Sŏ is referring to the way that Hegel, in his *Philosophy of History*, narrated the unfolding of world history and world spirit from the "Oriental World" (China, India, and Persia [111]) to Greece, Rome, and, finally, Germany. This is an example of the spatialization of time, the plotting of regions on a spatialized time line of historical development. This view of history was very important in the Japanese Empire, including in the works of one of Sŏ's primary references in this essay, Kōyama Iwao.

3. This translation is taken from Lau, *Tao* (5).

4. This translation is from Lau, *Analects* (146).

5. This translation of Zisi appears in Legge (297). I have added to the sentence to make it clearer that Sŏ is quoting Nishida, who is quoting Zisi, who is quoting the Master, who is quoting an ode.

6. Here I translate 민족 (*minjok*) as "people" because East and West are not nations but rather peoples with shared cultures. I have used "nation" in the other cases of the term, although its meaning generally hovers between "nation," "people," "ethnicity," and "race."

7. The Chinese characters of the Korean term for object, 대상 (*tae-sang*), mean "opposing shape."

8. The classical Sanskrit term *atman* means "self" in English. Sŏ translates *atman* into Korean as 我 (아; *a*) and transliterates it as 아트만 (*at'ŭman*).

9. Sŏ adds in parentheses the Chinese character for negation, 否 (부; *pu*), after each transliterated "*neti*" (네치; *nech'i*). The Sanskrit phrase *neti neti* is usually translated as "not this, not that."

10. For an explanation of the origins and significance of the distinction between the practical subject, 主体 (*shutai*), and the epistemological subject, 主観 (*shukan*), in modern Japanese philosophy, see Sakai 78–90. These terms are translated respectively as 주체 (*chuch'e*) and 주관 (*chugwan*) in Korean.

11. Sŏ cites the Zen Buddhist doctrine of 不立文字 (부립문자; *purimmunja*), or "revelation without dependence on words," but changes 文字, or "words and letters," to 文学 (문학; *munhak*), referring to literature. The doctrine asserts a break from any reliance on scripture and an intuitive and practical enlightenment gained through embodied training and negation.

12. Sŏ echoes Hegel's readings of the symbolism of art in the Orient as less developed than classical and modern European expressions of beauty (*Hegel's Aesthetics* 323–426).

Literature and Ethics

Humanities Critique (인문평론; *Inmun p'yŏngnon*)
October 1940
Colonial Korea

1.

Since ancient times, various theories concerning the essential function of literature have been passed down. However, the most encompassing and straightforward perspective seems to view literature as one form of human understanding.[1] One can see Aristotle's *Poetics* as an early and consummate example of the perspective that literature is a type of understanding. "It is, moreover, evident from what has been said that it is not the function of the poet to relate what has happened, but what may happen—what is possible according to the law of probability or necessity. . . . The true difference between the historian and the poet is that one relates what has happened and the other what may happen. Poetry, therefore, is a more philosophical and a higher thing than history: for poetry tends to express the universal, history the particular."[2] This means that the essence of literature, like history, lies in understanding the human but differs from history in the method of understanding.

If the essence of literature lies in understanding the human, then the value of literature must be that it expresses the trueness of the human. The purpose of understanding is generally to investigate the trueness of thought. Without the act of differentiating what is true and what is false, and making judgments, understanding would have no distinct function. In this sense, the essential function of literature is no different from that of science.

However, this does not necessarily mean that the trueness that literature pursues must belong to the same dimension as the trueness that science researches. Furthermore, if the trueness that is literature's goal were neither greater nor lesser than the trueness of science, then, frankly, we would not seek, independently from science, a distinct method of understanding called literature.

How, then, do literary trueness and scientific trueness differ? Contemporary conventional wisdom is that scientific trueness generally satisfies lawfulness and necessity and indeed must do so. When one speaks of trueness in science, one means something lawful and necessary. However, that which is lawful in science is understood in literature as something characterological, and that which is necessary in science appears in literature as something destined. If the trueness spoken of in science expresses something lawful and necessary, the trueness spoken of in literature generally expresses something character-ological or destined. Furthermore, if law and necessity are concepts that indicate some kind of truthfulness, character and destiny are concepts that imply some kind of authenticity. Here I think we can call the trueness that is the goal of science simply *truth*, as suggested by the term *scientific truth*, and call the trueness that is the goal of literature simply *authenticity*, as suggested by the term *literary authenticity*. We commonly state that we "do not know if it is the truth because it does not feel authentic" or that "one person's authenticity is not the truth of all people." There is some risk in the terminological resemblance between these phrases in the way that they emphasize only the analogous aspects of truth and authenticity; one must also point out the differences between their meanings. As we know from these phrases, when we refer to truth we usually mean trueness in a particular conceptual form, and when we refer to authenticity we mean trueness in a particular ontological form. As opposed to the former, which generally exists as an objective and universal form, the latter is discovered in a subjective and individual form. Just as enunciations of truth can be seen in the laws or formulas of science, enunciations of authenticity manifest themselves in propositions about persons, such as the personalities and characters of literature, even though those propositions generally appear to be impersonal statements. The specificity of truth lies in breaking away entirely from human subjectivity, moving into the rational world of the self and taking on an ascetic character, and then demanding universal validity; on the other hand, the specificity of authenticity lies in settling down in the sensible world, taking on a sociable character, and demanding universal validity rather through the deepening of one's connection to human subjectivity.[3] The trueness that science seeks is the truth of such a form, and the trueness that literature seeks is in the authenticity of such a form. Truth and authenticity differ in the character of their being, and therefore our attitude toward each of them must also differ. In relation to truth we normally require the precision of objective verification, but in relation to authenticity we require a depth of practical subjective experience. The former requires accuracy, whereas the latter requires solemnity; the former requires certainty, whereas the latter requires sincerity. In other words, scientific truths must satisfy the demands of the intellect, but literary authenticity must satisfy the demands of righteousness in addition to those of the intellect. This is why literature, more than science, can have a high degree of solemnity and sincerity, even when it is somewhat flawed in its precision and accuracy.

When truth and authenticity are posed as opposite extremes, cases in which they do not overlap also arise. For example, an illusion of water imagined by a thirsty person cannot be true, but its authenticity must be acknowledged;[4] likewise, the proposition of non-Euclidean geometry that two parallel lines will eventually meet cannot be authentic, but its truth cannot be denied. However, is it possible that something authentic that does not imply truth should be referred to as a subjective fact rather than as something authentic? Events such as a thirsty person's illusion about water or someone's dream about flying around naked are certainly one kind of psychological fact that we experience, even if they do not have a universally valid, actual necessity. Conversely, when we say that something is authentic, this can only mean a trueness that implies truth, even if this sacrifices the usual terminology in some respect. Although they differ in the character of their being, truth and authenticity certainly express an identical trueness in facts. Truth is the trueness of facts, and authenticity is also the trueness of facts. Therefore, truth and authenticity must have internally some kind of necessary connection. In other words, truth that is not corroborated as authenticity cannot be truth in its highest sense, and authenticity that does not imply truth cannot be authentic in a genuine sense. Literary authenticity, on this basis, must correspond to scientific truth, as an identical understanding of fact.

What kind of connections, then, do fact, truth, and authenticity hold? I think that empirical facts, scientific truths, and literary authenticity belong to different levels that each hold logical connections, negating and being negated by one another, subsuming and being subsumed by one another.

First, facts are the various specific and vivid phenomena of everyday life, provided as the primary material for the understanding. Specifically, they are psychological facts, material facts, and practical facts; they are direct, contingent, and individual. However, truth negates the contingency and individuality of these various facts and uses a conceptual sign to express the objective essence and necessary connections that penetrate and tie together the interior of a collection of facts. The particularity of truth is that it is abstract, universal, and necessary. Isn't authenticity, then, the unity of fact and truth, a concrete universality and concrete necessity for which truth has negated again its own abstract universality and abstract necessity and returned to being practical subjective fact? Authenticity that implies truth is universal and necessary like truth, but unlike the universality and necessity of truth, which are deindividuated and abstract, authenticity's universality and necessity are rather individual and concrete like facts. In other words, if literary authenticity is that which sublates scientific truth into practical subjectivity, then calling it by Kim Namch'ŏn's phrase "personal truth" is correct. We can now recognize that the trueness of literature, which is a trueness that exists at a higher level than science, must contain within it the trueness of science, and the trueness of science, to become literature, must be elevated to the level of human authenticity.

If we observe the contemporary literary situation from this point of view, there is a clear reason why one group of critics has traditionally treated the tendentious literature of the past as a mere extension of social science or as a literature of concepts. Literature in which ideas roam around unclothed inside the work can be neither a literature of truth nor a literature of authenticity. In the tendentious literature of those days, objective truth was unable to intensify into a practical subjective morality. In this sense, the humanist literature that appeared in response to this tendentious literature welcomed serial literature that pursued authenticity, including the literature of authenticity by luminaries such as Fyodor Dostoevsky and André Gide; this was a necessary course and one whose contributions we cannot ignore. However, this trend progressed to an extreme and eventually led to the importation of the irrational ethical thought of Lev Shestov and Søren Kierkegaard, which caused a commotion of debate for a while. But if truth cannot be what is true in literature, can authenticity be the genuine literary trueness? Of course, this is not a question for Dostoevksy and Gide, who were imported then, but a question for the literature of the here and now. That which is genuinely authentic would shed the skin of the past while containing its kernel of truth. If truth is that which has the power to satisfy all humans and their demands, then literature that disregards such truth will certainly be unable to provoke in us a solemnity and sincerity of feeling.

2.

However, if the trueness that literature seeks corresponds to authenticity, it is closer to ethical trueness rather than scientific trueness. If ethics seeks the trueness of the ethical, it is usually easy to focus our common sense on the maxims and virtues of practical morality in the everyday life of the human being. However, the primary task does not actually lie there, but rather more broadly in elucidating the social and acting human. Herein was Hegel's motivation for developing, in his philosophy of right, a theory of the state and economy as the content of ethics. Not only political and economic life but also the entire social life of the human carry meaning as ethical fact. This is self-evident. The social action of the human is more than a relation between things or a relation between subject and object; it is a human and expressive relation between subject and subject, between *I* and *you*. The expressive activity between subject and subject certainly implies some kind of social meaning. Of course, within so-called instrumental existence one sees the relation between the subject and a thing, and this has meaning. However, using Martin Heidegger's terminology, the negotiation between subject and tool is a relation of concern (*Besorgen*), whereas the negotiation between subject and subject is a relation of solicitude (*Fürsorge*). The meaning implied by solicitude is the attitude, comportment, body, and manners—the so-called disposition of ethos—that we have when we face another person. However, the matters of literature and the matters of ethics differ in quality and scale. In other words, the matters treated by literature are the social relations of action between human and human and therefore carry various social and ethical meanings. Some contemporary critics state that the task of literature is to describe the "spiritual custom" of one era and one society, to report on a period accurately. Yes! The task of literature is precisely to suggest the human trueness or moral trueness of an era and a society through the description of their spiritual customs. Spiritual custom, put in more precise terms, means the ethical substance commonly expressed in German philosophy with the phrase "objective spirit." In English and French, ethical substance is a way of differentiating the historical character of generations, eras, nations, and societies according to their respective spiritual conventions. In this way, the social value of literature lies equally in proposing the human trueness or ethical trueness of an era, a generation, a nation, or a social class through the description of ethical customs that differ in character according to history and society. Furthermore, ethical action is a human negotiation between subject and subject, or between *I* and *you*, and has a human and expressive character that differs from the movement of an object, the motion of an animal, and, of course, the activity of the negotiation between humans and objects. Furthermore, the subjective and expressive action of the human has the self-conscious characteristic of an identity of inside and outside, which makes an external call become an internal response and an internal call become an external response. In an ethics concerned with the subjective and expressive action of the human, a material trueness, or an objective trueness, cannot be trueness in its full meaning. Just as social, expressive action is related to the human and the subject, its trueness must have a subjective and human authenticity. In other words, ethical trueness is not just objectively true but also must be subjectively authentic. Of course, even if the ethical maxims of a certain nation and era circulate universally as things that are "true" for that nation, when they lack the human authenticity provided by a human acting within that nation, responding to these maxims internally and autonomously, then they have already lost their value as ethical trueness. When the actions that we undertake in the name of the various ethical maxims of a society become ethical, we cannot ignore the requirement of practical subjectivity, a foundational presupposition. This is the reason that conscience and common sense are problematized so vociferously in ethics. As we can understand here, that which is ethical is also human. There is nothing ethical that is not also human. If elevating and growing the human nature of the human is a technology of ethics, the so-called ethicality that makes ethics be ethics must certainly be a human quality. In ethics, then, trueness means subjective authenticity and human authenticity. Wasn't the literary trueness sought by literature, and described earlier, such a subjective and human authenticity? The trueness sought by literature is nothing other than ethical trueness. It is not only that the matters treated in literature are ethical facts but also that the trueness that literature seeks is inseparable from ethical authenticity.

3.

According to the above, ethics, first, is all the social rules, methods, and orders that govern the attitudes and actions between humans as social and collective beings, and, second, can only be ethics when each action undertaken in the name of the various norms and orders, as subjective and expressive actions, have the proper and called-on disposition demanded by an autonomous social conscience and common sense internal to the human. Thus, when we discuss ethics, we must consider two of its aspects. One is the conventionality of ethics (*Sittlichkeit*) and the other is the feelingness of ethics (*Moralität*). All the national and civic orders—tradition, habit, law, rite, cultural products, and systems—that define the rules and regulations of action in the collective everyday life of human society belong to the conventionality of ethics, whereas the practical reason, humanity, conscience, and common sense that provide subjective authenticity to these social conventions all represent the feelingness of ethics. The national and civic orders are the various social norms that have already been systematized and conventionalized and that are expressed in phrases like national morality, civic morality, household morality, and public morality; practical reason, humanity, conscience, and common sense are all the moral demands

made in accordance with a pure formal law of autonomous and universal free will belonging to one human, as
we can discover in the most definitive theories of Kant's
moral philosophy. Practical reason, humanity, common
sense, and conscience, looked at historically and phenom-
enally, develop and emerge within social convention.
Nonetheless, beyond the conventions from which they
emerge, they function independently, and each requires
human sincerity toward social action.

Now, if we oppose convention and feeling to one another as two extremes, feeling is internal, in contrast to
the exteriority of convention, and is subjective, as opposed to being substantive. If convention is something
historical, then feeling is something natural, and if
convention is related to content, then feeling is formal.
Thus, the conventionality of ethics can have external restrictions, whereas the feelingness of ethics cannot but
hold an internal sense of duty. Or rather, convention has
a fixed and stable inertia, whereas feeling has a nastic
movement that does not adhere to anything external or
formal. Therefore, convention easily hardens into something systematic or nomothetic (artificial) that compels
obedience and coercion, but feeling, if it combines with
something impulsive and physic (vital), can transform
into an ethics of creation and innovation. Convention
is transmitted and historical and begins and ends in the

particular, but feeling is universally human and is simultaneously individual and has universality. Convention is innate to a closed society and has a centripetal and cyclical quality, but feeling is innate to an open society and has a centrifugal and directional quality. In this sense, if convention is the ethics of nation and the ethics of class, feeling is the ethics of individuals and the ethics of humanity.

However, when we discuss ethics in the genuine sense of the word, it is neither simply conventional nor simply felt. Ethics definitely forms as a convention of social life and develops historically. The ethics of a given era and a given nation always has a particular historical character and social content. Without this kind of particular and substantive system of conventions, distinct ethics would not exist. However, ethics as mere convention has a direct, totalitarian structure that precedes the individual and is a prearranged social and national ground through which we form ourselves, from the day we arrive on earth, as only one limb of the totality.[5] The ethicality of ethics and the humanness of the human can be established only subsequently to the establishment of individual self-consciousness. It has been a repeated proposition until now that when our actions have no antagonism between subject and subject, or between person and person, they have no ethical meaning. Even viewed from the limited perspective of social life, it is impossible for a certain social system to maintain its existence solely through external restrictions and sanctions such as the legal system and its ordinances. Along with this kind of external order, the formation of a social and ethical *Gemüt* that can support the ground of the order is necessary. In other words, if an order is established, an ethical self-consciousness about this order among all the members is necessary for it to continue to exist. Ethical self-consciousness about the collective life of society is what makes each member belonging to a totality transform the external demands of that totality into their own internal demand. Therefore, when there exists no so-called expressive self-consciousness through which an external call becomes the internal mission and the internal mission becomes an external call, the external emphases of the totality cannot command the spontaneous obedience of each member. Ethical consciousness must bring about the establishment of an individual who negates the hypocritical totality by way of their experience of consciousness. What emerges is an ethics of feeling, the so-called breaking of convention. However, the opposition between individual and individual is possible only under the presupposition of the collective existence shared between individual and individual. The ethical consciousness that begins with the establishment of the individual must reach its end through the sublation of the individual. Ethical substance in the superior sense occurs when the totality returns from division to unity again, through its establishment and then sublation of the individual.

In other words, social, ethical substance in its genuine meaning is neither mere convention nor simply felt. Ethical substance is the unity of convention and feeling, so humanness must permeate every corner of convention, and convention must exist for ethical substance as an expression of humanness. Furthermore, as shown above, ethical substance can be actualized only through the dialectical unity of the totality mediated by the individual. Ethics in its genuine meaning is practical subjective ethics as the unity of the epistemological subject of feeling and the substantiality of convention; it is concrete universal ethics that unifies the particularity of convention and the universality of feeling. Particularity can only attain universality through the mediation of the individual and the universal can only become individual through the mediation of the particular. The historical content of convention can only fulfill the requirements of subjective authenticity by combining with the formal laws of feeling, and the formal laws of feeling can only satisfy the demands of objective actuality by combining with the historical content of convention.

It is a happy society and a happy era that attain perfect harmony between feeling and convention through the ethical substance of a society and accomplish in their ethics the complete unity of content and form, history and the human, substance and subject, particular and universal. Such an era and such a society exist very rarely and have commonly been absent in the long histories of various nations. This kind of perfect ethical substance can only be actualized in an era that has achieved symmetry and harmony, with no gulf between a society's base and its superstructure and no deep conflict between social classes. In summary, this kind of actualization of ethical substance is only possible during a period in which a society transcends the stage of destruction and unrest and promises classical and pastoral development toward construction and completion. Furthermore, as we can see in the epic poetry of classical Greece, the literature that emerges during such an era and describes its social life can produce a perfect model of humanness that grasps the moderation and equilibrium through which spirit and body, convention and feeling, individuality and sociality, and a hero and the people are completely united (on this point I reference Ch'oe Chaesŏ's publication from last month, "Epic, Romance, Fiction"). There is no other possible cause for this: in Greece at that time social conventions and individual feeling obtained a perfect internal

harmony, and the humanness of all the members of society was able to promote health and cheerful growth
without suffering from distortion or injury. The ethical
trueness sought by literature in such a society must be
an ethos that circulates contemporaneously among the
people of that period, because the operative ethos must
not only objectively maintain its truth and historical
rationality but also subjectively have human authenticity. Historical rationality has a concrete and universal
quality and refers to the fact that the particular and the
universal are not divided within certain social systems
of certain eras and that the social system always has the
necessity to continue to exist historically. And, of course,
such a social system must have historical rationality and
involve subjective authenticity. The unity of convention
and feeling does not break apart, and the social system
does not lose its human authenticity. If ethical trueness is
objectively truthful at the same time as it is subjectively
authentic, then the ethical trueness of an era in which
convention and feeling have formed a perfect unity is
nothing but the ethos passing through that era contemporaneously. Thus, the operative ethos during such periods must appear both in literature and in the morality of
the authors themselves, and writers will not be conscious
of a distinct morality other than this operative ethos.
The spirit of the writer belongs entirely to that era. The

eccentric lives that contemporary writers take up in opposition to their own time would be a matter of indiffer-
ence to writers living within the happy ethos of such an
era. These latter writers have no reason to distrust or to
doubt the era in which they live. For a writer who does
not doubt the era in which they live, there is no basis for
developing a consciousness of eccentric living. For such
an era and society, literature conveys the ethical trueness
of the era; however, it may not be easy for literature to
do so in the present.

4.

The ethical substance of society, as more than life (*Mehr
als Leben*)—to borrow a term from Georg Simmel—
establishes its own system and therefore has innate logic
and laws; and in opposition to more life (*Mehr Leben*), it
also has an internal inertia that blocks the progress and
development of life.

   Each ethical convention and each maxim have a fixed
form; as stated above, they are immobile and inflexible
and have a conservativeness and fixedness that allow
them to retain their forms. On the other hand, life has
fluidity and transcendence, constantly advancing and
developing into "more life," as both the before and the
beyond of fixed forms. Life always gives rise to a living

person or something that has lived. The vitality of life always discards old things and gives birth to new ones. In contrast to the way that the objective order, or the other-form of life, determines and solidifies itself, humanness, or the self-form of life, constantly creates and rejuvenates itself. If the ethical substance of "more than life" is the form of life, then the humanness that is "more life" can be seen as the content of life; if the former is the limit of life, then the latter can be seen as the flow of life. Although the ethical order of society appears as an objective expression of life at the foundation of its existence, if it is to give itself a fixed form, a gap and opposition must emerge between its fixed and established tendency and the creative and fluid desire of the human. Life attempts to break away from the established ethical system and advance, and the ethical system attempts to break away from itself and contain passing life in the system's fixed form. If the centrifugal tendency of life is enhanced, then the centripetal action of the ethical system also strengthens. Through the division of the totality and the sublation of the individual, convention and feeling, which had returned to harmony and unity, transition again from harmony to conflict and from unity to division. Content and form, history and the human, particular and universal, and substance and subject divide into abstract antagonists. Each ethical maxim and order that has cre-

ated an even development of humanness transforms into
a fetter against the development of humanness. Ethical
maxims and orders discard their function as the subjective ground that until now has subsumed the human,
and transition to an intellectual position that provides an
objective barrier against the human. An ethics that has
taken this course and arrived at the stage of being in conflict with humanness must subjectively eliminate human
authenticity, at the same time as it has already objectively
lost its historical rationality. Historical rationality is truth
that has a concrete, universal disposition, but the particular that divides from the universal must be something
irrational; if human authenticity is subjective authenticity, then both the substance that is separated from the
subject and the history that is separated from the human
are definitely inauthentic. In other words, such an established ethics has lost ethical trueness and therefore does
not move past the sedimentation of ethics and habits
belonging to a simple framework that has forfeited true
ethicality. Nonetheless, despite the sedimentation of
frameworks and habits, such an ethics has tremendous
power to bind and whip humanness, which calls for a
new life and new ethics in actuality. The humanness that
develops under the restraints of a schematic ethics will
inevitably suffer from the contradiction between convention and feeling and will become distorted, atrophied,

injured, and ill. There forms a humanness that lacks harmony and moderation, and it becomes deflated and foolish. Body and spirit, intellect and righteousness, psyche and action, and individuality and sociality lose their balance and unity and fall into despair; an unhealthy and unsound human is born.

In what kind of era are convention and feeling opposed in the ethical substance of society and the historicity and humanness, particularity and universality, of divided ethics? If a society can pursue perfect harmony between convention and feeling when it has moved beyond the stage of origination and unrest and entered a stage that promises classical and pastoral development toward construction and completion, then the breakdown of such a harmony seems to occur in periods when this society has moved beyond the stage of construction and completion and has entered the stage of unrest and anxiety. If the stage of development toward construction and completion allows one to anticipate an era in which the tendency for unity within a society is predominant over the tendency toward opposition, the stage of unrest and anxiety is a phenomenon that we see during periods when the tendency toward opposition is predominant over the tendency toward unity. In periods when gaps and oppositions manifest between all the strata and processes that construct a society, one cannot hope for any harmony between the *Sitte* and *Gemüt* of ethics.

What shape is taken by the humanness expressed in the literature of such an era of anxiety and unrest? As we can see in contemporary literature, the literature of such an era creates a humanness that is distorted and for whom body and spirit, psyche and action, intellect and feeling, and individuality and sociality have lost their balance and harmony. The human of excessive action who appears in André Malraux's literature, or the humans of too much psyche that we see in the literature of James Joyce, Marcel Proust, and others, are one contemporary form of the human. However, even setting aside such characteristic and typical forms of the human, in contemporary literature we can find various flawed human images, from perverse individuals who lack any adaptability to social life to mechanical humans who lack all individuality. Within a life for which *Sitte* and *Gemüt* are in conflict, it will be difficult to form a complete humanness that can control in a unitary fashion each affiliation between multifaceted actions. Not only that, but the psyches of the humans living in such a life and era, and particularly the psyches of writers, will also be more incomplete than complete, more imbalanced than balanced, more lacking in stability than having stable feeling; they will be prone to action more than to stillness, excess more than moderation, unhealthiness more than healthiness, perversion more than integrity, vulgarity more than refinement—in a word, they will be more Dionysian than Apollonian and will be more attracted and fascinated by contemporary rather than classical things. Isn't this the reason that people today are drawn more to the dynamic and content-oriented beauty characterized by instability and imbalance, and action and excess, rather than to the mathematical and formal beauty that characterizes the harmony and stillness, and the stability and outline, that we see in classical Greek art? If the psychological characteristics of the contemporary human are such, then when readers approach works of literature by contemporary writers in which form and content are woven together strangely, they must have the feeling of viewing a kind of Leaning Tower of Pisa. The characters that appear in such works certainly carry a sort of stability and balance into the midst of instability and imbalance and convey to the reader's psyche a sense of energy and pressure that differs from the sense of peace and grace that we feel with classical art. However, in the present as well, we can hope to find such qualities only rarely, in magnificent works. This kind of internal form, which we find only in modern art, has already collapsed in contemporary art. (In contrast to the monodimensional stability and balance that are characteristic of Greek art and that we can call *external form*, the multidimensional stability of instability and balance of imbalance that are characteristic of modern art can be referred to as *internal form*, borrowing a term from German aesthetics.) The phenomenon of the collapse of fiction, which is a problem in contemporary literature, can be seen in this light. The collapse of fiction occurs alongside the collapse of the internal form which was the tradition of modern art; as stated above, when we view this as a socioethical problem, the collapse originates from the divisions and distortions of humanness that are born of the contradiction between *Sitte* and *Gemüt*.

Another important characteristic of literature from an era in which the *Sitte* and *Gemüt* of ethics have lost their unity is that no self-evident ethical trueness has been given to its writers. In other words, not only are the objects of description in literature human images that lack a perfect harmony, but there is also no self-evident ethical trueness in the will of writers or in the ethics that they seek. Each of these problems has an intimate connection to the other, serving as its premise and its conclusion. The ethos that passes through this era is already a particularity that has divided from anything universal and something historical that has separated from anything human. A mere particularity that has divided from the universal cannot have historical rationality, and a simple history that has separated from the human lacks in human authenticity. In other words, such a particularity has objectively lost its truth and subjectively lost its authenticity. As stated above, if we can see the ethos that lacks historical and human authenticity as a mere practice bereft of ethical qualities, then it is also difficult for this ethos to become the morality of writers. And if it is difficult for writers to accept as is the established ethos of an era, then they must seek a new morality and a new ethical trueness. It is natural that when writers cannot see the given ethics as self-evident trueness or self-evident ethics, then their attention turns to the creation of a new ethics. The fact that a writer does not accept as is the ethics of an era is evidence that their spirit exists eccentrically, in opposition to the era in which they live. If they are content with a satisfied feeling about the era in which they live, they have no reason to be suspicious about the ethos of that era. We can imagine that in eras that lack unity of *Sitte* and *Gemüt*, the body of the writer may live in that era, but their spirit migrates to a world of past memories or future hopes. In order to alleviate this absent consciousness, the *Sitte* and *Gemüt* that were first divided must return to unity.

However, separation and conflict between *Sitte* and *Gemüt* signifies that a society has entered a stage of anxiety

and unrest, and this anxiety and unrest express out-
wardly the internal contradictions in the social organs.
Returning *Sitte* and *Gemüt* from division to unity and
from conflict to harmony requires that the basic organs
of the society, which are the material foundation for its
ethics, be reorganized on a new foundation that can
sublate their contradictions. This means that history is
transitioning from one social formation to another and
that ethics is transitioning from one moral system to another. The logic of movement in ethics is also the same
logic of movement in society. Just as society's return
from division to unity is not a mere cyclical return to
an older form but is realized through the development
to a higher form, the return of the *Sitte* and *Gemüt* of
ethics from division to unity is also realized through the
transition to a higher *Gemüt*. In other words, this movement does not mean the reproduction of a simple ethics of the past, and it must announce the birth of a new
ethics. And I think this kind of process of movement of
ethics follows the internal structure of morality; it begins with a division of the totality that is mediated by
the part and ends with a return of the totality through
another negation of this part. Morality that is static in
the position of a holon (a particular universal) is sublated
into an ethics that has both concrete and universal historical rationality and objective, subjective, and human

authenticity; and this sublation must occur through some kind of establishment and sublation of individual, universal subjectivity.

However, there appear to be two paths toward overcoming the conflicts between the strata of a society, when viewing the form of the phenomenon broadly. Besides the path of eliminating them from below, there is the path of synthesizing them from above. Looking at the present historically, it appears to be a time of anxiety and unrest; contemporary totalism, then, can be seen as one political formation created to overcome from above these conflicts of society. However, as contemporary totalism demands unity from above, it must acknowledge the absolute superiority of the unity of the totality against the opposition of the part, as we can see in many states today. It is a situation in which the significance of every single historical convention passed down from the nation's ancient ancestors must be held in esteem as a necessary means toward unity. In these states, dependence on good and bad conventions of feeling increases in concentration and therefore the discrepancies between the two become more serious. One feels that every civic action of every member of society at some point abandons its essence as an action between subject and subject and becomes an activity between object and object, an incarnation of mere convention. One feels that the human here acts more as persona than as personality. The reason for these feelings is the same: in such states, regardless if each national convention is an old thing or a new thing, the *Gemüt* internal to the human that ultimately practices this convention is neither this old thing nor this new thing innate to the physical makeup of that convention. This *Gemüt* belongs neither to a feudal ideology of rank nor to a contemporary ideology of function and is quite suited to a modern temperament. In other words, some would say if contemporary totalism also seeks to resolve these contradictions between *Sitte* and *Gemüt*, and between history and the human, it must cultivate an ethical *Gemüt* that belongs to its own physiology. Yes! For contemporary totalism to exist as a new order, it requires an ethical *Gemüt* that belongs to itself. The fact that the ethics of the new system and the new ethics of the economy are being posed as problems in the current debates taking place in Tokyo is due, I think, to this same requirement. However, as we can see in the above argument, we cannot forget the following point. Namely, what I call the ethical *Gemüt* organizes the world of the internal feelings of the human and therefore must have individual and universal characteristics rooted in humanness and not be a mere particularity that pertains only to one nation's historical makeup. In other words, at the same time as the ethical *Gemüt* pertains to the historical makeup of the nation, it also pertains to the essence of the human. For an ethical *Gemüt* to be created, this society, whatever form it takes, must be an open world and not a closed place, a linear assembly and not a circular community. Is it necessary for contemporary totalism to create such an ethical *Gemüt*? If it is difficult to guarantee *Gemüt* when viewing it as the physiology of totalism, then it would be difficult to discover the illness of the contemporary human. This illness, as stated above, refers to the various divisive and spoiled tendencies of contemporary humanness, which emerge from the contradiction between convention and feeling. If the distance between convention and feeling is not resolved, then it is also difficult to overcome the absent consciousness of contemporary writers. The absent consciousness of writers means an existence concerned with one's own place. Therefore, the spirit that seeks the trueness of writers must evade the ethos of a single era and direct its focus to a deep and distant place.

That the spirit must pay attention to this distant place indicates that in a time like the present, when convention and feeling are divided, literature cannot grasp the authenticity of the present simply by describing the present ethos. If convention that is separate from feeling cannot have historical rationality and subjective authenticity, then there have to be clear doubts about whether we must seek the authenticity of the present in the current ethos. In this sense, it seems that the best direction for literature cannot be found solely through the kinds of things discussed by today's intelligentsia, such as the "urban nomad" or the "description of custom." However, between these two phrases, the "urban nomad" and the "description of custom," the first definitely refers to the mode of popular literature and the mode of the writer who accepts the current ethos as is, as their own morality, and describes contemporary customs from the standpoint of that ethos. The second phrase also refers to the description of customs, but in contrast to the first, it is able to go beyond the standpoint of the current ethos and describe customs from a distinct ethical point of view. This mode is realist literature. Here the writer of necessity directs their scalpel toward the dissection of the essence of contemporary custom and as a result appears to criticize contemporary ethics. All the ironies and paradoxes innate only to literature appear as a sharp means of criticizing customs.

If the description of customs becomes the criticism of customs, we must consider one important premise. Through the description of various contemporary customs, the eyes of the writer must pursue and focus on the manner and processes through which the humanness of modern people gets distorted and malformed as they move through the scenes of life. In other words, through a panorama of contemporary customs, the various abnormal conditions of development undergone by the contemporary human must come together into a single stream and appear clearly before our eyes. A description of an era's customs that is not such a panorama cannot become a criticism of the ethos of that era. Only when the emaciated and crushed humanness of modern people confronts the obese body of contemporary custom can the physiological reason for its obesity become apparent.[6] Writers who describe customs must always have the intelligence and shrewdness to direct their lens toward scenes of acute conflict between the contemporary ethos and humanness.

In this situation, too, speaking fundamentally, we should not forget that a writer's true motivation for describing customs is the pursuit of the essence and tendencies of contemporary humanness, rather than there being significance in customs themselves. Because only through describing customs can the genuine appearance of the human be thrown into relief. If the essence of literature lies in the pursuit of human trueness, then isn't the most important thing to describe customs in order to research the human, rather than to confront the human for the sake of custom? In this sense, we must locate the significance of the description of customs in seeking the existential aspects and developmental trends of the contemporary human. I use the term *contemporary human*, but we know that this term includes many stratifications. Viewed superficially, humanness can be characterized by simple concepts such as distortion or growth; however, considering its other dimensions, and though it remains distorted, humanness also has, in a social sense, a primary mode of existence and implies, in a historical sense, a single direction of movement. The sprout of a new ethics can only be grasped through the pursuit of the various social-existential aspects and historical-developmental trends of the human strata, which make up the contemporary ethos and its odd contrasts.

In any case, human ethical authenticity is what literature seeks. Therefore, the ethicality of literature must also establish the authenticity of the human. The ethicality of literature is its raison d'être. The writer's duty must be dedication to authenticity and the defense of authenticity. However, in attempting to dedicate themselves to authenticity, contemporary writers must confront the entangled diametrical oppositions of contemporary ethics and humanness.

Notes by the Editor

1. For the translation of this essay, I referred to the original publication in *Humanities Critique*; see Sǒ, "Munhak."

2. This translation is from Butcher (35).

3. Throughout most of the essay, Sŏ uses the term 주체 (*chuch'e*) to refer to the practical subject of action, the main concern of this essay. However, in this sentence, "human subjectivity" is a translation of 인간의 주관 (*in'gan ŭi chugwan*). In this instance Sŏ uses the term *chugwan*, or "epistemological subject," to refer to the contemplative human subject of science. I have translated both *chuch'e* and *chugwan* as "subject" or "subjectivity," distinguishing between the two with "practical" and "epistemological" only when necessary. But the nuances of the two terms should be kept in mind and reference should be made to the Korean text.

4. Sŏ's example of a thirsty person imagining water is a reference to a debate between Im Hwa and Kim Namch'ŏn concerning Kim's short story "Water." Im Hwa argued that the story lacks class consciousness and historical subjectivity and is too focused on physiological and psychological details ("Yuwŏl"). Sŏ defends Kim's idea of "personal truth," although his idea of literary authenticity calls for the elevation of facts related to the individual to a higher level of universal moral truth and for the synthesis of authenticity with universal scientific truth through literature.

5. In this passage Sŏ begins his ethical criticism of "totalism" (토탈리즘; *t'ot'allijŭm*), repeating his more detailed discussion of its lack of individual morality in "Chisŏng." "Totalism" refers critically to the politics and culture of European fascism and the ethnonationalist strains of Japanese fascism. In his works on East Asia and the East Asian Community he pushed for the idea of a regional, multiethnic nation-state.

6. "Emaciated" and "obese" reflect the vocabulary in Korean. During this period writers often used imagery of fat bodies to refer metaphorically to the accumulation of wealth or power. Sŏ seems to mean in this sentence that modern people are impoverished and that only when powerful contemporary cultural customs are viewed in relation to that impoverishment can we see how these customs became powerful. I have included the sentence to stay true to Sŏ's original text but register here my disagreement with this type of metaphor.

Sociology of Nostalgia

Morning Light (조광; *Chogwang*)
November 1940
Colonial Korea

1. Idea and Ideology

Every time we encounter some way of thought or spirit, I think it is proper to consider at least two aspects in order to grasp it concretely.[1] First, we should grasp it as idea, and second, as ideology.

Of course, when we try to understand what thought is, or to understand thought from thought itself, it seems to have an ideational character. As one can see from the translated words 이념 *inyŏm* (理念) and 이상 *isang* (理想), the term *idea* indicates an eternal meaning-value, an expression of human will that a given thought implies.[2] If so, when we view meaning only as meaning and value only as value, we can understand that each thought points definitively toward an eternal meaning and a superior value. Because if the meaning and value of thought are not eternal and superior, thought loses its effectiveness as a political weapon that can grasp and guide the human.

Therefore, we can know the following: that no matter how weak the thought content might be, if we understand each way of thinking from an ideational perspective according only to the meaning that it implies, there is no thought that is both ugly and admirable. For example, humanity has come to look down on cases in which ugly actions are undertaken in the name of God or our neighbors, wearing the mask of admirable thinking.

We cannot distinguish the identity of thought by looking at thought only as thought. To distinguish the identity of thought, we must situate it within some kind of historical or social context and question its actual and social significance. In other words, the meaning that thought carries must be understood according to its meaning in relation to existence at the same time as it is understood according to its meaning as thought. Of course, it is not unimportant to know the outward meaning of thought. At the same time, we must also excavate by whose hand and for whom, and with what necessity and role, this thought arose. This is the perspective that views thought in terms of its so-called ideological character. Ideology refers to both a meaning related to existence and a meaning belonging to existence. If the concept of thought in itself is called idea, then the "concept as condition" that is grasped in relation to existence is ideology. Only when we view thought from this kind of ideological perspective does the actual and specific significance of each way of thinking appear clearly.

However, under today's circumstances, I think an ideational rather than ideological perspective is required in the evaluation of thought. Accentuating the ideological character of thought is what so-called critical intellect does and not something in which creative intellect participates. The reasons for an ideational perspective are simple. One important reason is that today is a period that requires action more than interpretation and problematizes planning more than understanding.

However, can there be true creation where there is no criticism, and can there be true action where there is no interpretation? If today's criticism is not connected to creation and today's interpretation is severed from action, then isn't this less a flaw of contemporary intellect and more a flaw of organization today, which does not offer opportunities for criticism and interpretation to engage in creation and action? In any case, creation and criticism, and action and interpretation, should in principle be unified. We know that an ideological criticism of thought may not necessarily have thought's ideational character, but if an idea born anew today has the essence of an idea in the superior sense, which is to guide an era, there is no need to evade it, even if it is a kind of ideological criticism.

2. Common Sense

The various factors that accompany people's evalua-
tions of common sense are peculiar. Cursorily speaking,
people have a tendency, on the one hand, to be grateful
for common sense and, on the other, to feel contempt
for it. For example, in relation to the former, the implied meaning of the phrase "that person lacks common
sense" is that common sense should be respected. However, conversely, the phrase "that person is too commonsensical" has the meaning that common sense is
contemptible. However, isn't the essence of common
sense hidden precisely inside this kind of dichotomous
evaluation of it?

Common sense expresses intensively the accumulated
experiences of human life of an era; it refers to the sound-
est and most uncomplicated perspectives that are commonly and generally in use. In other words, as that which
signifies the average standard of the culture that a given
nation has reached at a given time, common sense refers
to the popular viewpoints belonging to anyone who has
arrived at the average epistemological or moral standard
of that time. We know that during any era humans of
that time will always be required "to know at least these
things." The phrase "that person lacks common sense"
means that they cannot understand even those things

that everyone should or does know. On the other hand, doesn't the phrase "should know at least those things" also mean that "those things" do not constitute sufficient knowledge or action? To say someone is too common-sensical means that knowing only those things is not sufficient knowledge.

Here we can understand that at the same time as common sense is the minimum necessary knowledge, it is not the maximum sufficient knowledge. In other words, common sense is both necessary and insufficient knowledge.

The reason that common sense is both respected and derided surely comes from this epistemological characteristic of common sense. Perhaps common sense is respected because there are people who cannot achieve it, and it is derided because there are people who cannot surpass it. Therefore, shouldn't we discuss the nobility of common sense for the sake of those who have yet to attain it and discuss the weakness of common sense for those who are limited only to common sense? This is an attitude about common sense that common sense itself demands.

But how should we conduct this discussion? We look at examples of the ways that these requirements for common sense are commonly propagated in this society. On the one hand, those who would surpass common sense hide the notion of common sense as insufficient knowledge and therefore enshrine common sense like an ancestral tablet; on the other hand, those who cannot attain common sense ignore the notion of common sense as necessary knowledge and therefore disdain common sense as something old and worthless. There is not much of a problem if those who are insensitive to the requirements of common sense are individual, common citizens who do not have significant connections to the lives and destinies of other people. However, if these people are in the position to influence the lives of many other people, the pitiable ones are those people who must follow behind. The most pitiable case is those who get distanced from common sense by those who should be the most commonsensical.

3. The Metaphysics of Nostalgia

One word that we commonly use is *nostalgia*. Nostalgia is a type of sorrow, a pathos related to one's home. However, sorrow, as a sentiment that accompanies the operation of memory and as the content of its representation, always arises through the desire for events or things that once existed in the past and have already been lost in the present. However, in principle nostalgia is an emotion that can be held only by people who have left their home or by people who have lost their home.

It is customary that we use *home* to indicate the natural rural region where we began and spent the time of our youth. If in its primary meaning home refers to that which "thickens our flesh and bones," then of course it refers to this kind of natural climate that serves as the cradle for our bodies. Therefore, our sorrow is also largely connected to this natural climate. Because of this connection, the climate of one's native place always appears as a mnemonic representation deep in the heart of a person captured by nostalgia. This is the case not only for a single individual but also for an entire nation. Even today the home of the Jewish people remains Palestine, and the landscape that appears within their nostalgia remains the desolate nature of Palestine.[3]

However, if we use the term *home* symbolically, then we go beyond the bodily home discussed above and see that a spiritual home also exists. There are times when, even as our body lives settled in the climate in which we were born and raised, our spirit alone feels the emotion of nostalgia about the spiritual things of a specific period (or country) that has already passed. Friedrich Hölderlin's spiritual home was Greece, and J. W. Goethe's spiritual home was Italy. Why is that? If there is a time of youth for the body, there is also a time of youth for the spirit, and if a determined natural climate is required as the necessary environment for the growth of the body, then wouldn't there be a determined spiritual climate that is the necessary environment for the growth of the spirit? We know that from the day their individuality awakens, humans, whoever they are, will each have only one cradle of spirit that will embrace their young individuality and impart to them ideals and passion for future humans. However, there are likely to be frequent ups and downs and substitutions during periods of rapid movement in the "accent" of history, in the thought, morality, customs, atmosphere, and so on that make up the spiritual climate of a given era. When the world of spirit that organized the earliest days of our lives collapses, and the distant and distinct spiritual customs connected to that world enter the past chronicle of our lives, the world of spirit that has already collapsed comes to possess the character of a kind of lost home for our spiritual-historical life and comes to evoke a kind of nostalgia each time we remember it. Even if we look at just the intellectual class of this land, they no doubt grew up within the natural landscape of this land, but their spirits grew by wandering through a series of strange spiritual worlds that resulted from the scholarship and art belonging to the European genealogy. Because the cradle of their spirit was from the beginning different from the cradle of their bodies, since the day they came into the world it was difficult for their spirit to establish complete harmony between their bodily dispositions and the indigenous spiritual climate of this land. Today this long distance has become even more severe, and through the entrenchment of an incommensurable spirit, the spiritual environment of this land has become extremely rough and narrow. Therefore, even just looking to our everyday feelings, we know that it is not unreasonable to discuss here a home for the spirit along with a home for the body and to point out that there are two distinct origins for nostalgia.

However, if we think one step ahead, are the homes of which we can speak limited to the bodily home and the spiritual home discussed above? If I am to move on to discuss the metaphysics of nostalgia, I think I must now be able to go beyond the two homes discussed above and finally hypothesize what I call the primal home. What does this mean? Since ancient times many poets have viewed the universe as a guesthouse and their lives as a passing through. This is a concept of home that lumps together the whole world and regards it as solely a foreign place, and it comes from the comprehension that thinks of the human as a solely exilic being.

Of course, this is not a way of thinking that is limited only to the sentiments of a few poets. The metaphor of life as a journey is a deeply rooted concept that has passed throughout the world and has been harbored by every person since ancient times. In Buddhism, the world is viewed as a temporary dwelling, or as this world as opposed to the next, and in Christianity it is the place of trials and charity between the Fall and arrival at judgment. It is said that the world is only "this world," but where is the preceding world that is not this world? And if the history of humanity began with the Fall, was there no place where humanity lived before the Fall? Not only that, but we also commonly say that the human "comes out" into this world, meaning that it is born, and that it "returns," meaning that it dies. If our having been born in this world is not simply survival but "thrownness," then of course there should be a place from which we came, and if our dying is not simply death but a return through death, then of course there should be a place to which we return.[4] I would like to call this place from which we come and to which we return the primal home, based on the *khora* that F. W. J. Schelling called primal history. Why call it home? Because humans' comprehending their birth as a coming out and their death as a return through death means that they comprehend this world in which they live as a foreign place and their survival as exilic survival. That the human comprehends this world and its own survival in this way, as an exile or a passenger, can only mean that the place from whence we came and to which we return is our home. Furthermore, this is a home before this world and not something within this world. And the home before our spiritual home or bodily home must carry a primal and fundamental meaning for whatever comes after it. In this sense, we should call it literally the primal home. A human life refers to the short time during which some-one leaves the primal home and appears, wanders in this world, and then returns to that place again. If so, isn't it logical that we have nostalgia, too, for that primal home! We might even say that Plato's envisioning of a world of Ideas and John Milton's poetic imagination of a paradise from which we are banished came to fruition, in a cer-tain sense, out of this kind of nostalgia.

However, put more precisely, the primal home is not really something that exists for us in the same way as the bodily home. Thinking about it this way would amount to mystical thought or a priest's sermon. It is not logical that the preceding world would exist in the same way as this world, and there is no reason that paradise would ex-ist in the same way as the world on earth. What we are discussing here is simply a problem of the human's self-comprehension and a phenomenological interpretation of human existence that takes human self-comprehension as a hint.

However, if the human fosters a particular comprehension of its existence that considers it to be fundamentally exilic survival—just as the human's view of life as a journey is one fundamental mode of comprehending its own survival—then the emotion of homesickness, or nostalgia, must be one original emotion for the human. Of course, nostalgia will unquestionably be one of the human's basic emotions if all humans live with a consciousness of exile, however small or large (that we cannot clearly cognize our consciousness of these eccentricities at all times is because they only pass by buried under secular existence). Because nostalgia is a basic human emotion, not only have many poets sung of it since ancient times but it also constantly appears with renewed emotional effect as an eternal theme of more recent poetic works. If humanity cannot be fulfilled without something like a primal home, such as what was traditionally called Eden or the world of Ideas, and this is a result of the human's existence being exilic survival, then religious poetry and conceptual poetry are also expressions of the originary and eternal nostalgia that the human harbors. In other words, the human being is traditionally the starting point of every instance of nostalgia and has a fundamental and somehow primal nostalgia-ness. Of course, this nostalgia-ness does not refer to what we commonly see in the Christian thought of the West:

that the human, because it was banished from paradise, is forced to live a life on earth bereft of a native land. What we call paradise or the world of Ideas are one or two noetic forms of the primal home. Therefore, the nostalgia related to them is already prescribed by a specified object. What we are calling the primal home refers to the possible ground for nostalgia beyond all such limits. Doesn't the nostalgia that captures the emotions of poets usually lack a specified object and rather have such an ambiguous yet fundamental essence?

If so, then why does nostalgia constitute the originality of humanness in such a way? If the fundamentality of nostalgia is due to the human comprehending its survival as exilic survival, then the conditions that make possible this kind of comprehension of existence by the human are certainly the key to clarifying the fundamentality of nostalgia. However, the human can comprehend its survival as exilic survival because it is a being that always exists transcendentally in relation to the place and environment where it lives. If the human were a being like an animal that was only immediate and immanent to its environment, then there would be no reason for the human to become conscious that it came into this world or that it left a home where it once lived in the past. And the reason that the human can transcend its environment is that it is a being that can by nature transcend itself. If the human were not conscious of its present self as both *I* and *oneself*, then wouldn't the human also not have the ability to know its present environment as *one's own* and its past environment as *mine*? Therefore, if we try to figure out the foundation that constitutes the fundamentality of nostalgia for the human, it originates in the human's own transcendentality.

However, what is described above is, so to speak, the philosophical-anthropological ground for nostalgia, not its sociohistorical ground.[5] A phenomenon such as the inundation of nostalgia in a particular society or era must be treated not only as a human phenomenon but also as a social phenomenon. And the ground for nostalgia as social phenomenon can only be understood through the analysis and elucidation of each objective and historical condition and circumstance of a certain time and a certain society. The contemporary period is excessively inundated with nostalgia. Every manner and form of nostalgia is the mist filling the psychic void of contemporary humans. So-called travel literature or escape literature in the West also has at its foundation the nostalgia of people who have lost their home. When we see simple nihilism among the people exploring the deserts of Africa or the forests of the East, we are not seeing both sides of human psychology. Their nihilism arose because they could not be content with the contemporary environment of their

place, Europe. In other words, it is a void of the psyche
caused by the loss of a native land that would content
them. The people who have lost a native land that would
content them change the place where they live, because
they are unable to suppress their feelings toward some
kind of ambiguous native land that they carry in their
heart and that might satisfy their spirit. Therefore, being
wrapped up in a nostalgia that they cannot suppress is
the basis of their nihilism. The situation is no different
here. The nihilistic tendency that dominates the literature of this land also leaves behind the present moment
and is connected to a psyche that continually expresses
sorrow for past things and gropes for new things. As I
have just stated, the various objective significances of this
contemporary psyche must be elucidated and understood
in relation to the various historical conditions of society
today. It is not my purpose here to theorize these social
bases for contemporary nostalgia, so there is no need to
touch on that aspect of the problem here. However, if
nostalgia is one kind of expression of the human psyche's
consciousness of absence, then the inundation of nostalgia in the contemporary period expresses that all the conditions and circumstances of today's society have been
arranged such that in general the contemporary human
must survive exilically in relation to its own place. And
if in general the exilic survival of the human emerges

where there is some kind of crevice between the feelings of the human and the various spiritual customs that establish the conceptual basis for a society, then this situation must signify that this society has arrived at a stage of anxiety and unrest. There lies an important problem.

Notes by the Editor

1. For the translation of this essay, I referred to the original publication in *Morning Light*; see Sŏ, "'Hyangsu.'"

2. 理念 (이념; *inyŏm*) is usually translated as "concept," and 理想 (이상; *isang*) as "idea." Sŏ is pointing to the use of the character 理 (logic, rationality) in both words.

3. Sŏ's assertion of Zionist ideas about the significance of the Palestinian landscape for the Jewish people reveals some of the contradictions and problems in the writer's critique. Sŏ states that nostalgia has a physical connection to a natural landscape and climate, although the Jewish Diaspora would largely not have that connection with Palestine. He also describes nostalgia as an effect of universal exile. Such a turn to an ideology of naturalized roots in the face of exile is a typical mode of nostalgia conducive to nationalism and colonialism, and one that he does not critique thoroughly enough.

4. I have chosen to translate 出生存 (출생존; *ch'ulsaengjon*) with a term from Heidegger, thrownness (*Geworfenheit*). Although these characters are not the standard translation of *Geworfenheit* in Japanese or Korean, like Heidegger's term, Sŏ's term points to the existential condition, rather than the mere biological fact, of having been born into the world. As in Heidegger's works, for Sŏ, questions of home and origin arise out of this primary thrownness into the world.

5. See "Note on the Translations" and endnote 3 in Paik Ch'ŏl's essay "The Era of Human Description" for explanations of my choice to translate 인간학 (*in'ganhak*) as "philosophical anthropology." Here Sŏ uses the adjectival form.

ŎM HOSŎK

Ŏm Hosŏk (1912–75) was a socialist activist and literary critic. He was born in Hongwŏn in South Hamgyŏng province. In 1929, in his third year at the Hamhŭng Normal School, he was identified as having connections with the Kwangju anti-Japanese student protests and was expelled. He went to Tokyo as an exchange student and studied mathematics, but he soon quit school and returned to Korea. In 1931, while he was working in the fishing industry, an association formed to re-establish the Hongwŏn Red Peasant Union, and he joined it. He worked on the standing committee and in the education or cultivation (교양; *kyoyang*) section of the union in the village of Chuik. Then he became the chairman of the Noha district, before getting arrested by the Japanese police. In January 1933, he was sentenced to three years in prison at the Hamhŭng regional court.

When he was released from prison, Ŏm went to Seoul and studied literary criticism. After the end of World War II, he served as the lead writer of *Art* (예술; *Yesul*), the journal of the Federation of Korean Literary Arts in Hamhŭng. He then became the vice chairman of the Hamgyŏng provincial committee of the North Korean Federation of Literary Arts. In 1947, he did work in Pyongyang connected to the publication of

Cultural Front (문화전선; *Munhwa chŏnsŏn*) and *Literary Arts* (문학
예술; *Munhak yesul*), organs of the federation. In the 1950s, he
continued to write essays on culture and cultivation like the
one included here, supporting the purging of Kim Il Sung's
political and cultural rivals, including Im Hwa and Sŏ Insik.
In the 1960s, he was the chairman of the criticism section
of the Korean Writers' League. He became one of the most
important critics involved in the construction of the personality cult of Kim Il Sung, writing hundreds of essays with titles
such as "The Form of General Kim Il Sung in Korean Literature" ("조선문학에 나타난 김일성장군의 형성"; "Chosŏn munhak
e nat'anan Kim Il Sung changgun ŭi hyŏngsŏng"; 1950) and
"The Great Comrade Kim Il Sung's Thoughts on Correctly
Uniting Socialist Content and National Form" ("사회주의적 내
용과 민족적 형식을 옳게 결합할데 대한 위대한 수령 김일성동지의 사
상"; "Sahoejuŭijŏk naeyong kwa minjokchŏk hyŏngsik ŭl olk'e
kyŏrhaphal te taehan widaehan suryŏng Kim Il Sung tongji ŭi
sasang"; 1970).

The Problem of Typicality
in Literary Composition

The Aims of Literature (문학의 지향; *Munhak ŭi chihyang*)
1954
North Korea

1.

Despite all the falsehoods and dissembling of the aesthetics of formalism meant to deny the social function of literature, one of the clearest conclusions that the tradition of realism in our literature and its experience give to us is that the artistic value of a literary work is measured according to the degree to which it serves to cultivate the people.[1]

When the realist writers from the past linked the problem of the cultivation of the people to their creations, they became great for the first time, and their works were transmitted to future generations over a long historical period as something immortal. In the innumerable works by realist writers of the past, not only were the circumstances and the important social problems confronting the people of the writers' time reflected, but because of the moral judgment that these writers applied to the circumstances and social problems of the people, their works were also always consistent with the spirit of cultivating in the people a noble moral character with good intentions, keen wisdom, active will, and so on. There is no further need to state that the more that these problems to which writers apply their moral judgment in their works are connected to the mood and understanding of the people, the greater will be the works' significance for the people's cultivation. Such a work does not cultivate only the people of the writer's time but also serves the cultivation of the working people in our own time.

In Korean literature of the past, the creations of the New Tendency Group[2] cultivated in the Korean people bravery toward life and hope for a bright future through the writers' impassioned humanitarian judgments about the urgent social problems that these writers raised for the sake of liberating the Korean people from the dismal circumstances of Japanese rule, particularly starvation and a lack of rights. Coming to the period of Korea Artista Proleta Federacio (KAPF; the Korean Federation of Proletarian Artists),[3] the writers of this organization had a clearer and more active character, clarified the root causes that gave rise to all the social misfortunes of the Korean people, and cultivated in the people the thought of a liberation struggle that would release them from these misfortunes.

However, the realist literature of Korea's past cannot be a genuine realist tradition for our literature if it only cultivates the people of its own time and if in our time we research fixed historical eras, not benefitting from the power of these texts to provide help nor their power to cultivate value for the working people's life and constructive industry. Nonetheless, stating this problem at all certainly causes a smile. Why? Because a work of literature, in so far as it is realism, must reflect some aspects of the central problems in the life of its era, and these central problems also draw great interest from us today and offer abundant resources for the problem of the cultivation of the people.

The superior realist works of the New Tendency Group and KAPF, by exhibiting in front of us today on a vivid canvas the true picture of the past life and struggles of the Korean people of the 1920s and 1930s, not only arm us with correct knowledge about the life and struggles of our people at that time but also no doubt inspire the struggles of our working people today and provide immense strength to them through the revolutionary spirit and patriotic thought shown in the process of our people of that time struggling to liberate themselves. And if all the superior works of realist literature from the past still preserve their artistic value in the present, it is because these works assist in the cultivation of today's working people.

The fulfillment of the cultivation of our people in our own time by superior realist literature of the past is possible only by the power of artistic generalization and the embodying of that power in the typified forms standing at the center of works. Typified forms are the artistic expression of the typical phenomena of life or the personification of the important and essential things among the phenomena of life, and within these forms the important sociohistorical phenomena chosen by the writer are generalized into concrete and individual shapes. Readers come to receive the cultivation of knowledge concerning definite sociohistorical phenomena though these typified forms. Therefore, the process of the writer fulfilling the cultivation of the people through their works corresponds to the process of artistic generalization that creates typified forms within their works.

The core writers of KAPF turned their attention to the revolutionary advance of the Korean laboring class as the most important sociohistorical phenomenon of their time, and they guided their compositions and created typified forms of positive protagonists with the purpose of cultivating in the Korean laboring class its noble revolutionary talents and moral character. It is apt that they

turned to cultivating the centrality of their own concerns in the working people, generalizing in defined individuals, or typifying in defined types the revolutionary
process of how the sons and daughters of the fledgling
Korean working class could cast off and emerge from the
heavy yoke of Japanese rule and enter the shining path of
revolutionary struggle and how to fight against class en-
emies and stand at the head of the struggle for liberation.

In cultivating the working people, what the core writers of KAPF asserted in their creations—in other words,
the ideas that appeared in their works—was more than
anything a new moral character and revolutionary talent characterized by an iron will and hot-blooded, youth-
ful passion for arousing the revolutionary advance of
the fledgling Korean laboring class, enmity toward the
enemy and unwavering faith in victory, and a spirit of
heroic sacrifice and a bright and cheery optimism that
trusts in the future and loves life. These writers regarded
all the characteristics that have been developed into the
refined character and talent of our working class as the
most important phenomena in the future development
of the Korean people of that time and insisted on and
supported their development and growth, making these
characteristics the pathos[4] that guided their pens, and
making their duty the creation of positive protagonists
who personified these new refined characteristics of the

Korean people. And precisely this duty became a distinguishing sign of the serious differences between, on the one hand, the advanced writers assembled in KAPF and, on the other, the writers of the miscellaneous decadent tendencies of all bourgeois literatures, such as naturalism and formalism.

Im Hwa, who was recently revealed to be a heinous American spy, Yi Wŏnjo and the sectarian Yi T'aejun, Kim Namchŏn, and so on, walked a terribly different path from the core writers of KAPF, alongside all the bourgeois reactionary writers. Any reader who has even a small amount of knowledge about the Korean literature of the past knows that when the advanced writers of KAPF described the valiant, bright, optimistic nature of the positive protagonist in their superior works, which cultivated and assisted the working class, these writers conversely disguised incidental and individual phenomena as though they were typical phenomena, while trying to win over uncharacteristic elements such as the imbecilic spirit of defeat and despair, an abandonment of faith in victory, and an aversion to life.

Im Hwa, who has been shown to be a wicked American spy, judged the past revolutionary struggle of our working class as fated to be defeated; in doing so he viewed the work of the dedicated fighters as only meaningless and useless sacrifice. Therefore, while lecturing to the working class to put down their weapons, he presented the figure of the revolutionary fighters taking their tragic final steps. We can see the most representative example in "My Brother and the Brazier."[5] In this work, to clarify the typical phenomena and processes in the revolutionary struggle of the Korean working class, Im did not burrow underground and tried to propagate the idea of the fated defeat of the working class by presenting one-sidedly only uncharacteristic phenomena, such as fighters getting arrested by the Japanese police and walking righteously on the path of sacrifice, instead of presenting the genuine face of revolutionary fighters in the struggle. "My Brother and the Brazier" begins and ends as a statement of a righteous sister who embraces a broken clay brazier that was left behind by her older brother, a revolutionary fighter who was arrested honorably and whose future she laments. The broken clay brazier that is left behind righteously is not just a symbol for the destiny of the revolutionary fighter who is its owner; it becomes Im's conclusion about the destiny of the working class. Why? Because the revolutionary fighter in "My Brother and the Brazier" stands in for the destiny of the whole working class.

When the core writers of KAPF were cultivating the working youth in the thought and will of liberation struggle by describing the advanced form of revolutionary fighters in their works, Yi T'aejun, conversely, always described the filthy images of sexual perverts going mad in a world of carnal desire to remove the working youths from the liberation struggle and to direct their attention away from their concern for all of society's problems toward another place; furthermore, in "Night Journey," instead of guiding laborers who were disconnected from life toward the clear path of struggle to return them to life, he went ahead with a foreboding distortion about the destiny of the Korean working class by having them walk a night journey of despair.

Kim Namch'ŏn, in "Toward Youth," maligned our fighters of the laboring class during the era of Japanese rule by presenting the figure of the socialist who betrayed life and sank into the mire of futility and self-abandonment and then by misrepresenting this as the fate of all socialists.

One must state that confirmation of this concise example is the fact that when the core writers of KAPF from the same era described the figures of the genuine representatives of the Korean people, supporting and foregrounding the most important and essential aspects of the life of the Korean people and therefore its most typical aspect, the liberation struggle of the working class, at the same time the American spy Im, along with Yi T'aejun, Kim Namch'ŏn and so on, came to resist the liberation struggle of the Korean working class by describing one-sidedly only the incidental phenomena of the liberation struggle and, as we see with Kim Namch'ŏn, the figures of defectors from the revolution who are cursed and hated by the Korean people. In other words, our concern is that instead of portraying the important and essential aspects of the life of the Korean working class and within the liberation struggle, they conversely portrayed inessential things and pretended as though they were essential and typical.

It is ridiculous to negate the act of describing negative phenomena and characters. There is value in describing in more artistic works the figures of defectors from the revolution and the hatred they receive from the Korean people. In this case, the advanced writers of the past supported the struggle of the Korean working class and had definite, firm, and positive ideals and convictions—and carried out the duty—to help this class's future development.

The defector that Kim Namch'ŏn described in "Toward Youth" has no commonalities whatsoever with the disclosure of negative phenomena by advanced writers such as the above. The fact that Kim and others portrayed the negative figure of the defector without any positive conviction or ideal on the other side concerning the positive phenomena that are opposed to the negative phenomena that they portrayed means that the purpose that they pursued is to show that such defectors are a typical phenomenon in the revolutionary struggle of the Korean working class. The aim to absolutize one-sidedly the incidental and individual phenomena that arise in the process of the struggle of the Korean working class, without presenting the positive ideals and convictions on the other side, is a tendency of vulgar naturalism, the reactionary purpose of which is to distort actuality and authenticity and anesthetize the consciousness of the masses.

For writers, their standpoint and their tendency are determined according to what they regard as typical, what they affirm, and, conversely, what they negate among the complex phenomena of life. In other words, the tendency and party loyalty of writers are expressed in the turning of their attention to what kind of phenomena in life are socially significant and will become an impetus for the development of society, and their insisting on and emphasizing these consciously.

Therefore, at the Nineteenth Congress of the Communist Party of the Soviet Union, G. M. Malenkov stated that the typical is the basic area where party loyalty manifests. The fact that our advanced party has turned its attention to typicality proves how important a party task the problem of typicality has become for writers' cultivation of the people.

2.

The problem of typicality is one of the most complicated and important aesthetic problems. Concerning typicality, some people in the past have limited it to only those general phenomena that have been most widely spread, most often repeated, and sufficiently verified in life. However, if we limit typical things to those that are most widespread and general, and if we acknowledge that the minority of individual phenomena that are not widespread express the essence of a singular sociohistorical situation or point to characteristics that most sharply clarify some kind of sociohistorical process, then we are presented with the question of whether we can call these latter phenomena typical. Marxist-Leninist aesthetics has provided a correct answer to this question. As Malenkov stated in his report at the Nineteenth Congress of the Communist Party of the Soviet Union, "In the Marxist-Leninist understanding, that which is 'typical' does not mean, after all, some kind of statistical average. What we call 'typicality' is in accord with the essence of the sociohistorical phenomena of the times and does not simply refer to the phenomena that are most disseminated, most often repeated, or emerging daily."

The figure of Yi Mongnyong, the protagonist of "The Tale of Ch'unhyang," presents a good example in this regard. The figure of Yi is not a general figure that was common or widespread in the feudal society of the Chosŏn period. On the contrary, in the environment of the feudal ruling class governed by falsehood and immorality, the figure of Yi had an individual and exceptional existence. The fact that Yi comes into conflict with the very feudal ruling class that was the environment that raised and cultivated him, and that he tries to break away from it and bears hostility toward the status system that divided the *yangban* and the people, must be a rare, particular phenomenon that did not arise often.

Then what reason do we have to call Yi Mongnyong a typical figure? Yi, who is in conflict with his own environment because he has fallen for a commoner's daughter, is said to be "a prodigal son who came from the *yangban*," but that is not all. Not only does the conflict between Yi and his environment express sharply an omen of the disintegration of the decaying system of feudal *yangban* rule, the emergence of a figure such as Yi already expressed clearly the contradiction between the *yangban* ruling class and the people. In other words, one can say that the figure of Yi was most essentially revealing the process of collapse of the feudal *yangban* system of rule. The fact is that even though the figure of Yi was exceptional in his own environment, and in that sense was particular and individual, he nonetheless became someone typical.

This circumstance does not mean that all individual phenomena are atypical. It means that there are individual phenomena that cannot reveal the essence of any social process, but there are also individual phenomena that do so perfectly. Characters such as Yi Mongnyong represent this kind of individual phenomenon. As I state above, even though they are rare in number, they become extremely typical figures because they express the process of collapse of the feudal ruling class. Conversely, we cannot say such a thing regarding the description of figures of defectors from the revolution. There is no mistake that defection from the revolution is an individual phenomenon in the whole story of the developing revolution. However, this individual phenomenon, as a one-sided description of the revolution, does not clarify the essential process of the revolutionary struggle—in other words, the developmental process of a revolutionary struggle growing and moving forward; it cannot be something typical, and likewise, as a phenomenon in literature it must be called naturalism and not realism because it distorts the revolutionary struggle into a process of collapse. The example of the above-stated work of Kim Namch'ŏn is precisely this. This kind of individual phenomenon can become typical only when it serves the description of positive phenomena chosen to elucidate the victorious developmental process of the revolutionary struggle, or if not, when it is revealed under the sunlight of the ideals of a writer who supports the revolutionary struggle. In other words, a negative character can become the object of a realist description only on the condition that the writer emphasize and insist on a positive figure set up in conflict with the negative character who opposes them and who is described as a source of satire in a positive sense.

In summary, neither the class betrayal of Yi Mongnyong nor defection from the revolution is a general phenomenon. They are identical in that they are individual phenomena, but because the former is in accord with the essence of the feudal ruling class as a collapsing force and best expresses it, it can become a typical phenomenon, whereas for the latter, because it is not in accord with the essence of the advanced laboring class as a force of forward development, we know it can only be a one-sided description of that development and also cannot become any sort of typical phenomenon. Here we can see more clearly examples of the naturalist distortions that emerge when each phenomenon is described independently and not in relation to other phenomena. As with Yi Mongnyong, this has significance for the past. Until now discussions of the typicality of people were limited solely to the widespread types and the new types of our time. The types that were widespread in a past society controlled by social immorality and hideousness were represented by characters like Pyŏn Hakto[6] and appeared most frequently in critical realism, serving the purpose of the writer to criticize the old system ruled by such hideous people. On the other hand, there are also characters of the ruling class who betray their own class environment. In Russian literature, characters such as Leo Tolstoy's Anna Karenina (from the novel of the same name) and Mikhail Lermontov's Pechorin (from *Hero of Our Time*) represent figures similar to Yi Mongnyong in Korean literature. Maxim Gorky called these figures "prodigal sons of the ruling class," "white crows," or people "expelled" from their own class. These figures have to seem atypical when they are viewed from the perspective of the people of the past, and they might suggest that only the most widespread phenomena are typical. However, even though these figures were exceptional in their own time, by expressing most sharply the essence of the ruling class and the necessity of its process of collapse, they become sufficiently typical phenomena.

Types that are not disseminated, like we see in the example of Yi Mongnyong—in other words, those nonuniversal types not to be confused with the new types of our era—are very important for understanding the problem of typicality. Of course, new types are also types that have not yet been spread or repeated in society. However, if the types that are nonuniversal developed within critical realism as types borne of the contradictions of the ruling class itself, and exposed the old system, new types are represented by the new humans that developed in socialist realism and germinated within the people's struggle for and construction of a new society. Support for and insistence on new humans and their development are two of the most important duties of the advanced writers who stand for socialist realism. These writers show the capacity to make things appear superior and stable in the present, but already passing into decrepitude and death, and make it the goal of their creations to insist on the growth of the new capacity that is born and develops from this death. The core writers of KAPF were just like that. These writers, no matter how stable the Japan-ruled society that they confronted may have appeared, judged that it was already hardening historically and getting decrepit, and to accelerate its extinction they exposed the system of Japanese rule and advocated and described something new, the revolutionary fighters of the working class, as their own positive protagonists. And through the positive protagonists of these revolutionary fighters, they cultivated their era. The significance of this cultivation lay more than anything in the fact that a new type, the revolutionary fighters, became a socially disseminated type. In other words, they pointed to and described revolutionary fighters as representatives and models for the Korean people, which by inspiring the magnificent sons and daughters of the Korean people toward revolutionary struggle accelerated the development of the revolutionary struggle of the Korean working class. For this new type in the period of Japanese rule, the revolutionary fighters, to transform completely into a widespread type, a fundamental revolution of society was necessary. This was realized through the 15 August liberation.

Liberation brought about the transformation of the type of the new human, who was not general and was in the minority during the past era of Japanese rule, into a universal type that was general, positive, and widespread in society. The laborers, advanced peasants, and members of the Union of Democratic Youth in our society are all heroes of this new era and positive protagonists who appear in our literature. Today the duty of our writers is to capture the refined spiritual talents and positive characteristics that have spread widely in our society and to create artistic figures that have the value of being able to become models and objects of imitation for people. However, these refined talents and positive characteristics have already become elements that form the visage of common people and are widely propagated and general. In the period of the last nine years since liberation, our people have been cultivated into humans with refined character through the party and the state, and through the Fatherland Liberation War of the last three years they have been trained ideologically and morally into humans with more superior talent. Severe hardships and our victory over them trained numerous common Koreans into heroic personalities and the word *Korean* proudly brought tears to the eyes of all the people of the world. It is an important and urgent duty of our writers that they develop the refined heroic character of the Korean people that emerged in the administration of the Fatherland Liberation War so that it is expressed in the achievement of postwar rehabilitative construction.

A figure that generalizes the refined characteristics that the common people have into the valuable individuality of one person belongs to a disseminated and universal type. What we call typical does not refer to something expressed as a statistical average, and it would be just the same to exclude these universal types from the category of type. Marxism-Leninism teaches that the typical expresses the essence of singular sociohistorical phenomena and does not leave out phenomena that are widespread and that change often. Why? Because not only are phenomena that are widespread and change often not typical in their expression of the essence of singular sociohistorical phenomena, but also the fact that they have been disseminated widely is a result of the development of new typical phenomena and therefore means a transformation toward a widespread and universal type of a new kind.

The creation of widespread and universal types has important meaning, not only for cultivating our era, but also for cultivating future generations by clarifying through the character of the common people of our era the superiority of our system, which is how much our new social system serves as an advantageous environment for the development of the individuality, capability, and talent of the human. The old social system based in exploitation became a vicious environment that destroyed and disabled people instead of developing their individuality, capability, talent, and character. Such an environment collides harshly with numerous fates and as a result the phenomenon of the individual meeting a tragic end is general and repeated often. The typical phenomena that the critical realism of the past revealed in reflecting its own era, through which writers criticized their own era, provides us today with accurate knowledge of the life of that time.

However, if we regard the universal type as a simple harmony of ordinary humans, this is also incorrect. Universal phenomena of a developing society are always the result of the development of new phenomena and do not refer to ordinary phenomena of some kind of backward standard or certainly to a majority.

Aiming at the description of banal things that lag behind and hold the majority and opposing the description of new things and their development are precisely the basic occupations of naturalist writers. For naturalist writers, the more banal and ordinary are the figures in the work, the more they are "typical," and therefore they insist that it is sufficient for one writer, for the purpose of their composition, to describe the first person they meet on their path of observation and that there is no necessity to design a story. And they deny the description of all heroic and positive characteristics by insisting that the more the first person they describe is banal and a character one would often meet on the corner, the closer the person gets to the statistical average that is the standard of typicality for them.

Among the peasants, immediately after liberation, people who had feudal hereditary customs and feelings for the old society made up the majority. In our fledgling literature immediately after liberation, there appeared the naturalist tendency for some works to describe ordinary peasants, who were the majority in the farming villages, from the point of view of the statistical average and thereby to represent them as ignorant and foolish humans.

Concerning the question of how to describe contemporary protagonists, Gorky states,

> Our heroes who live in reality, the humans constructing social-
> ist culture, are much nobler and grander than the protagonists
> in our novellas and short stories. Certainly, we must describe
> them more grandly and more distinctly. This is not only a de-
> mand of life but also a demand of socialist realism, which should
> be thought of hypothetically; hypothesis, or speculation, is the
> sister of hyperbole, or exaggeration.

These words of Gorky are pertinent to the circumstances
of our early literature, which allowed peasants to be de-
graded as foolish characters in works that, in making
mediocre and backward peasants their protagonists,
chose humans of an average standard and in the majority
(rather than turning their attention to the advanced peasants) because of an old point of view concerning typicality, and therefore these works did not have any kind of
artistic generalization or hyperbole to clarify distinctly
the advanced appearance of our peasants. However,
Gorky's words are not just pertinent to our early literature but are also appropriate to the present situation,
because today as well our literature is lagging behind
reality, and we see in some works that the protagonists
are described more poorly than real protagonists.

The protagonists of literature are described more
poorly than the protagonists of reality because writers

do not research the source materials of life deeply and then reconstitute them aesthetically. The aesthetic reconstitution of the source materials of life, or the artistic generalization of characteristic things according to one's choice of materials from life—this artistic generalization itself appears as a conscious exaggeration of figures. This artistic generalization of life materials, or the exaggeration of figures, moves forward through speculation and design according to the writer's daring imaginative power. In other words, only when a writer receives inspiration from life, is engulfed and moved by a definite pathos, and embellishes a figure in their soul can they create an artistic literary work. To describe a protagonist magnificently, as protagonists genuinely appear in reality, the exaggeration of the source material that has been selected is necessary. There is no authentic art without hyperbole, and we cannot even speak of any realism if we ignore the method of hyperbole. Furthermore, where there is no hyperbole, types also cannot be created. In typifying, the role of hyperbole appears more than it does anywhere in the selection and generalization of what is characteristic. A portrait drawn by the soul of a genuine artist is more similar to its source than a photograph that is an accurate reproduction of the real person because the portrait raises that person to a type by expressing on their face and embellishing the secret characteristics that are hidden in the person's interior.

Make no mistake, if people saw in everyday life the makeup, movements, and dialogue of characters in a play, they would treat these characters in life as crazy people. Conversely, if characters in a play reproduced accurately on stage the makeup, movements, and dialogue just as people do them in everyday life, the audience members would certainly yawn and turn their backs. Characters in the theater appear authentic, in so far as they can provoke the audience's sympathy and inspiration, because they create an artistic image in the minds of the audience members by performing their movements hyperbolically and intensely and emphasizing their makeup and dialogue.

Therefore, in life, actuality and authenticity are different. Even if a writer is slavishly faithful only to actuality and reproduces it with however much exquisite ability, this record is distinct from some kind of sculpture of life and is rather dissimilar from the facts described, because it is only a single canvas and does not remind us of other similar phenomena or connote anything essential among the many phenomena that coexist or that have general commonality. The writer can capture on paper what is closest to the actuality of life or the authenticity of life only when, to describe these life facts and illuminate and exaggerate what is characteristic about them, they remove the unnecessary parts and, using their past experiences, provide a design for the necessary parts and make them into a vivid picture. Actually, to fully make a person into a type by the kind of fabrication discussed above, an exaggerated figure aesthetically reconstructed and described will always resemble the person more because of its authenticity than will a photograph that duplicates the person as they are in actuality. *Genuine writer* does not refer to someone who records the phenomena of life, but rather to an artistic talent that knows how to make models by expressing the essence of actuality through powerful, bold, and creative fantasies and designs and by personifying in a type the characteristics that best clarify the nature of the protagonist. Fabrication: not only is it not in contradiction with life and authenticity, but it is also what makes them clearer.

Notes by the Editor

1. For translating Ŏm's essay, I referred to the anthologized version; see Ŏm. Because of the constraints of space, only the first two sections of Ŏm's essay are included, but they provide the main conceptual argument. Ŏm goes on to discuss more literary works of the late 1940s and early 1950s.

2. See the introduction for more on the New Tendency Group.

3. See the introduction for more on KAPF.

4. In the original Korean, Ŏm transliterates the Russian term for pathos, пафос (*pafos*), two different ways: 빠포쓰 (*ppap'ossŭ*) and 빠포스 (*ppap'osŭ*).

5. Im, "Uri oppa"; see also Im, "My Brother."

6. Pyŏn Hakto is the villain of the Ch'unhyang folktale. After Yi Mongnyong falls in love with Sŏng Ch'unhyang but cannot have a public relationship with her because of their different social classes, Yi moves to Seoul with his father to finish his education. Meanwhile, Pyŏn replaces Yi's father as the country magistrate and is a morally corrupt leader who imprisons Ch'unhyang when she refuses his advances and plans to punish her on his birthday. Yi returns to the village to punish Pyŏn and marry Ch'unhyang.

Ch'oe Chaesŏ

Ch'oe Chaesŏ (1908–64) was born in Haeju in Hwanghae Province. He graduated from Kyŏngsŏng Normal School number 2 in 1926 and entered Kyŏngsŏng Imperial University (now Seoul National University). He received degrees in art and English literature and completed graduate school while lecturing in the Faculty of Law and Literature. He traveled to London to study. Upon his return to Korea, he taught at Posŏng College (now Korea University) and the law school of Kyŏngsŏng Imperial University. In 1937, he founded the journal *Humanities Society* (인문사; *Inmunsa*) and the next year published a book of criticism, *Literature and Intellect* (문학과 지성; *Munhak kwa chisŏng*). From 1939 to 1941, he was the editor and publisher of *Humanities Critique* (인문평론; *Inmun p'yŏngnon*).

Ch'oe made his debut as a critic in the journal *Emergent* (신흥; *Sinhŭng*) in 1931, introducing the work of the English literary scholar A. C. Bradley. In the 1930s, he published many articles in *The Chosun Ilbo* (조선일보; *Chosŏn ilbo*) and *The Dong-a Ilbo* (동아일보; *Tonga ilbo*) on a range of topics, including tendencies in contemporary American and English literature, intellectual literature, criticism and science, the realism of modernist works, and the Korean literary establishment. After the beginning of the Second Sino-Japanese War in 1937, he collaborated enthusiastically with the Japanese Empire. In 1939, he proposed to form a group of writers who would provide support to the imperial army and was active in the election of the group's members. Later that year he wrote a record of the proceedings of a farewell ceremony for the imperial army. In 1940, he gave lectures on Japanese patriotism and the literary arts all around Korea. In 1941, he changed the name of *Humanities Critique* to *National Literature* (国民文学; *Kokumin bungaku*) and began publishing it mostly in Japanese. His major book-length work of this period was *Korean Literature in a Time of Transition* (転換期の朝鮮文学; *Tenkanki no Chōsen bungaku*; 1943), an excerpt of which is included here. On the brink of liberation in June 1945, he helped to found the Korean Press Patriots' Association and continued his active support of Japan until the end of the war.

Particularly after the establishment of the Republic of Korea in 1948, Ch'oe's nationalism shifted to Korea and the US war against communism. He helped to organize a rally of national cultural figures at Sigon'gwan Theater in December of that year. However, in 1949, he was imprisoned under the Punishment Law for Antinational Activities; the indictment was withdrawn because of a statute of limitations. He went on to teach at Yonsei University, from 1949 to 1960; Dongguk University, from 1960 to 1961; and Hanyang University, until his death in 1964. During his career as a professor, he was central to the establishment of English literary studies in South Korea, publishing many works on the history of literary criticism as well as translations of the works of Shakespeare and other English writers. His many books include *The MacArthur*

Sensation (매카-더 선풍; *Maek'a-dŏ sŏnp'ung*; 1951), *Introduction to Literature* (문학개론; *Munhak kaeron*; 1957), *History of English Literature* (영문학사; *Yŏngmunhaksa*; 1959–60), *Collected Criticism of Ch'oe Chaesŏ* (최재서평론집; *Ch'oe Chaesŏ p'yŏngnonjip*; 1961), *On Cultivation* (교양론; *Kyoyangnon*; 1963), and *Shakespeare's Art as Order of Life* (셰익스피어 예술론; *Syeiksŭp'iŏ yesullon*; 1963; English translation, 1965).

The Spirit of Cultivation

Humanities Critique (인문평론; *Inmun p'yŏngnon*)
November 1939
Colonial Korea

Cultivation is ultimately a problem related to the individual.[1] In that case, it is convenient to think that the individual is a kind of virgin soil. The process of development and farming, of claiming the virgin soil, planting a seed, giving it fertilizer, weeding, making a flower bloom, and making it bear fruit—this is cultivation. In English one ties together *development* and *farming* and calls them by one word, *culture.*

Culture and social stimulation are the seeds and the fertilizer for cultivation. Cultivation is formed wherever the individual breathes culture and develops and grows a variety of their hidden abilities. Therefore, the spirit of cultivation is first of all the spirit of solitude. Why? Because culture, which is the fruit and the seed of cultivation, is perhaps social, but in order to develop and incubate culture inside an individual, a long period of solitude is certainly necessary.

Goethe once wrote: "Talent is nurtured in solitude / Character is formed in the full current of human life." In this poem, the training of talent is unequivocally cultivation. Therefore, cultivation has an essence that is incompatible with group life. That the human must participate in some sort of group life as a social personality is natural, but it cannot gain cultivation in group life, because cultivation requires private time to sit back alone and read, meditate, and struggle mentally. Therefore, a common anxiety in contemporary civilized countries is how to create harmony between the cultivation of the youth and group life. When, after the days of youth, group life is so vital as to completely eliminate private time, cultivation cannot be advanced; in the following statement, Thomas Mann discusses a similar phenomenon in Germany: "The fundamental problem today is not knowing anything about cultivation in the sense of noble and heartfelt self-denial, personal responsibility, and personal struggle, and instead trying to gain ease for oneself within group life."[2]

It is a big mistake to think that therefore cultivation is a problem of the individual and that Mann's statement is individualistic. The problems of individualism and cultivation exist at different levels and are incomparable; if there is something that can be considered in relation to cultivation, that would be humanism. If humanism at its foundation protects and enhances human value, then it does not bring about a lack of individual cultivation.

If the spirit of cultivation is the spirit of solitude, then it is also, to some degree, the spirit of transcendence. At the same time as cultivation is initiated by social stimulation, if a process of secretly digesting it internally is necessary, then it is natural that one must take on a transcendental attitude toward actual life to some degree. Even when immersed in the middle of actual life, one cannot cultivate without leaving behind utilitarian concepts. Even if one is reading the classics, if this is done for the utilitarian purpose of preparing for an examination, then it cannot be cultivation in the true sense. Cultivation is possible only when culture is not a means and is sought as its own end.

Therefore, in a time when the whole of society is in a frenzy for the sake of utilitarian purpose, to some degree the cultivation of the individual cannot be supported. One example might be Europe during the Industrial Revolution, and particularly English society in the latter half of the nineteenth century. At the same time as the whole of society did not love truth and did not look back to spiritual values, and was in a frenzy only for material gain, cultivation also ended up getting buried in the soil. Matthew Arnold's famous theory of cultivation came about during this era. He called the specificity of the English "Philistinism." They tried to manage by custom and precedent rather than by scientific principles, to live by opportunistic adaptation to circumstances rather than by ideals, and to obtain worldly success and material gains rather than truth and beauty; against this approach he exulted the noble Greek spirit of light and expanse.

I am not saying that cultivation is completely useless socially. Only that cultivation cannot come about through the guidance of utilitarian concepts alone. Because the aim of cultivation lies in the free and harmonious development of humanness, how one should make it socially useful is a separate issue.

Occupational education and humanities education become problems at this point. For a nation, giving young people occupational training from early on and creating a basis for them to act as capable members of society right after they leave school is the duty of the state. However, if the education of minors is implemented only with an occupational perspective, we can assume that this is a worrisome problem for the complete development of national character. Because, after all, mechanical humans who exhaust the majority of their ability and develop only one specific capacity cannot usually constitute a healthy nation.

Because cultivation always prioritizes the complete growth of the individual, it is adept at development and avoids getting fragmented. So-called cultivated people and specialists are two concepts that do not coexist in a society like today's, where social differentiation has developed to an extreme. A specialist is a person who develops a particular skill in only one small facet, and if we compare them to the whole of the human, they are just a single machine. However, cultivation takes on a serious attitude of denial toward the mechanization of the human. It comes to touch each part of culture so that the human can develop harmoniously as a human. Therefore, cultivation cannot but be something general. But being general is sufficient. After all, the basic problems of human life cannot be resolved through the various analyses and research of specialists, but only by surveying the totality and passing unfragmented judgments about the whole situation.

The most important problem of today is probably how specialized education and general cultivation can coexist. Actually, how many examples can we point to of people who are scholars with worldwide authority within their specialized fields but concerning their general (basic) life problems are altogether no better than children? If we want to rescue contemporary civilization from its final ruin, there is definitely truth to the humanists' proclamation that there is only one way: to fulfill the general cultivation of the specialists.

The problems of humanities education and scientific education lie here. Humanities disciplines such as language, classics, history, ethics, philosophy, and so on are disciplines that have made cultivation their aim since ancient times. There are many problems when we ask if the various disciplines directed toward natural science that are taught in today's schools prioritize cultivation or specialized training. It is a fact that compared to the end of the eighteenth century in Europe, when these problems were the fiercest problems, scientific education has been cultivated, but we must recognize the fact that from a humanistic perspective the sciences have still not been sufficiently cultivated. In Europe, as well, science was still not cultivated until the first half of the nineteenth century. One can surmise it by taking as evidence the public criticism that arose in French society during the time of the works of naturalist writers. The naturalist novel's provocation of cultivated society of the time was due more to its specialized terms than its immorality. The descriptions of all the details about a character's occupation and environment were done with specialized terms, terms that the common reader absolutely could not understand. Victor Hugo offered a complete one-page architectural dictionary in *The Hunchback of Notre*

Dame and a maritime dictionary in *The Toilers of the Sea*. Readers lamented that if one wanted to understand Honoré de Balzac's *César Birotteau* completely, one had to become a lawyer or an accountant, and to understand some scenes from Émile Zola's works, one had to become a butcher oneself.

Modern people's knowledge about science has developed to a surprising degree, and specialized descriptions appear in novels without causing shock. However, whether this scientific knowledge contributes to the cultivation of a person is probably doubtful because modern people, as I state above, do not know how to make this science and knowledge truly useful for human value and because the great majority of scientific knowledge is practically useless for basic life problems.

Cultivation is inclusive at the same time as it is general. Cultivation is not exclusive toward culture of a certain disposition or a certain field of culture. The spirit of cultivation is first of all to absorb anything that is worth becoming nourishment for its individuality, even if it is heterogeneous. Therefore, a society that trains people from a young age to have an overly exclusive attitude toward foreign culture will not be a happy society.

We commonly see examples around us and among us of self-division and of individualities not being unifying because of too much absorption of heterogeneous culture. This is the greatest anxiety of modern people, and particularly for us, who sit in the East and import European culture; however, there is no change in the principle that the spirit of cultivation is a spirit of tolerance. Therefore, even if cultivation's diversity and its unicity of belief are two concepts that do not coexist today, there is an important duty for contemporary intellectuals to make them coexist.

A problem to be considered in connection with this issue is the relationship between humanism and religion. If, as stated above, humanism is the life attitude at the foundation of cultivation, then religion is a life attitude that centers on belief. Humanism touches diverse cultures and aims at fostering enriched individuality, and religion aims at training and focusing on individuality through unified principles. Therefore, when humanism and religion seek their goals along a single path, a clash between them will surely arise. We have seen this example many times in the past. However, when they are made harmonious with each other, there have also been eras that have established great civilizations. Thus we can learn the lesson that "humanism without religion is shallow and religion without humanism is narrow-minded." Another way to say this is that cultivation without belief is shallow, and belief without cultivation is narrow-minded. One can offer as actual examples cheap cosmopolitanism and completely stubborn Puritanism. If we look at them through the whole of the human, we cannot deny that both of these are incomplete forms.

In this way, when cultivation develops because of many elements entering it and mutually adapting, it has a harmonious state and will have lofty knowledge and right judgment about external society. Previous discussion of this appears in my essay "On Taste," and I will omit it here, but the one additional remark I want to make is that erudition and conscience are different issues.

Erudition is the accumulation of knowledge, and conscience is a critical power of discrimination indicating cultivation. We can gain erudition by reading books, but having erudition does not mean having conscience. Erudition is, after all, the accumulation of knowledge, and one can even borrow other scholars' knowledge verbatim, but because conscience is wisdom that only a long period of cultivation can instill, it cannot be borrowed thoughtlessly.

The sign of a cultivated person is that instead of brandishing their erudition at society they have a tranquil but exacting conscience and do not move blindly but have their own sense of value and critical standards through which to apply proper judgment. The spirit of cultivation is, after all, the spirit of criticism. And that is the most important point.

Notes by the Editor

1. For translating "The Spirit of Cultivation," I referred to Ch'oe, "Kyoyang."

2. My translation from Ch'oe's Korean.

What Is Poetic?

Korean Literature in a Time of Transition
(転換期の朝鮮文学; *Tenkanki no Chōsen bungaku*)
1943
Colonial Korea

It is reasonable that standards of beauty change along with transitions between eras; or rather, they must change.[1] Those who do not change are either incompetent people or else cowards. To the question "What is poetic?" I would like for contemporary poets to answer, "There is beauty in many people working for a single idea."

It is possible for beauty to be recognized in the actions or poses of individual children, but we feel something truly beautiful when we see all the children of a national school marching in file. A cooperative beauty is there that cannot be explained thoroughly with formalist aesthetic concepts like the beauty of order or of groups. Individual humans are demonstrating their own power to the greatest limit; however, they are by no means desirous. Because they are being conducted by one absolute idea, they show a majesty that has no individual plan, and in this a sublime beauty is produced. This beauty also differs from a formalist rhythmic beauty that arises from a wooden doll or machine that is only moving mechanically. There is a condition of strain between extreme repression and the demonstration of extreme life, and there shines forth an austere beauty that seeks only to scatter sparks. For that matter, one can say that modern warfare demonstrates the pinnacle of cooperative beauty. Sometimes I report glimpses of this in the pages of a newspaper, and I imagine that if I clarify the whole picture of, for example, an opposed landing carried out through the cooperation of land, sea, and air, then I have probably captured the consciousness of beauty of modern people. But it is sad how unexpectedly few works aim at such a cooperative beauty of war and are also successful at its expression.

However, the cooperative beauty of many people working for a single idea certainly does not occur in military training or war alone. In a more peaceful world, as well, there appears a solemn cooperative beauty in labor that is different from play. Because there is not a more suitable example closer in proximity, I will use a work by William Wordsworth. I think the example of "A March Poem," which begins "The cock is crowing / The stream is flowing," can be reevaluated as a work that exalts cooperative beauty. As a poem that describes the tranquil landscape of the countryside and the beginning of spring, it was quoted by middle school leaders, but I think this work has a more serious meaning.

> The cock is crowing
> The stream is flowing
> The small birds twitter
> The lake doth glitter
> The green field sleeps in the sun;
> The oldest and youngest
> Are at work with the strongest;
> The cattle are grazing,
> Their heads never raising;
> There are forty feeding like one!

Here there is also a beauty of rhythm coursing through the whole, but the beauty appears in what we could call the unity between rider and horse more than in that playful element, in silently being engaged in a single idea—production.

Lately it seems that Japanese aesthetics is researched enthusiastically, and I think that here the Japanese character of beauty can be extrapolated. In this case, the thesis that beauty is many people working for a single idea must be elevated to the thesis that it is people who have many ideas returning to one. To commit this thesis to mind, many precedents can be pointed to from the *Man'yōshū*.

> Our great Sovereign, a goddess,
> Of her sacred will

Has reared a towering palace
On Yoshinu's shore,
Encircled by its rapids;
And, climbing, she surveys the land.
The overlapping mountains,
Rising like green walls,
Offer the blossoms in spring,
And with autumn, show their tinted leaves,
As godly tributes to the Throne.
The god of the Yu River, to provide the royal table,
Holds the cormorant-fishing
In its upper shallows,
And sinks the fishing-nets,
In the lower stream.
Thus the mountains and the river
Serve our Sovereign, one in will;
It is truly the reign of a divinity.[2]

Because my knowledge of (Japanese) national literature is limited, I do not know very well, but I think that if one searched there would be a more appropriate work.[3]

Contemporary poets should open their eyes more to this beauty of unification. Rather than going around collecting fragments of decadent beauty in the ruins of individuality, shouldn't they direct their eyes toward the outside more and search for beauty in the unified customs that today are spreading everywhere, from the capital to farming villages? On this point, Kim Chonghan's essay "Concerning the Chorus" (*National Literature*, April edition), and in particular his recent masterwork "Custom" (*National Literature*, June edition), are bold in their design, but they succeed equally as literary works that go in a new direction.

Poets until now have largely searched too much for the beauty of isolation. They showed people running counter to the whole, separating themselves from the whole, and therefore showed an abnormal taste for opposition and ruination. Why do so many poems about vagabonds and fallen leaves appear in a typical anthology of poetry? This not only foments a mood of division and decay and is not interesting in terms of the unity of (Japanese) national thought, but there is also something unbearably deplorable about it as a way of doing poetry. It is, after all, the result of the final stages of individualism, and we must escape this pathological state as quickly as possible.

Notes by the Editor

1. For translating "What Is Poetic?," I referred to the version published in Ch'oe, "Nani." The essay has been translated from Japanese.

2. This translation of a portion of Kakinomoto Hitomaro's untitled poem appears in *Thousand Poems 29.*

3. I have translated 国民 (*kokumin*) as "(Japanese) national" here, with "Japanese" in parentheses, to indicate that Ch'oe is not referring to Korean literature but rather to the literature of Japan and all its national and colonial subjects.

The Idea of Literature

Literary Theory (문학원론; *Munhak wŏllon*)
1957
South Korea

Literature is a type of art.[1] Art can only be experienced by us directly. Literature has something in its inherent essence that resists the deductive prescription of concepts. This is why the majority of definitions of literature are limited to a litany of insipid abstract terminology.

However, it is not entirely impossible to experience literature—concretely speaking, read important literary works—and then try to form an idea of literature. Attempting to explain such an idea is the purpose of this book. Therefore, after the entirety of the book is read, it will have spoken about this problem. However, we must have a point of departure for this description. This point of departure will be discovered within the definitions of literature that already exist.

Below I will introduce the definitions of literature of various predecessors, not limiting myself to their simple enumeration, but classifying them systematically and dealing with them critically to some degree. If we proceed this way, I believe the questions that we must think about will emerge naturally.

1. Literature in the Broadest Meaning

The meaning of literature is letters.[2] (A person of letters is a *munin*.) Therefore, we can say that the meaningful arrangement of letters is literature in the most originary sense. Ancient people took a sharp tool and recorded writing on the inner bark of trees. The Latin word *liber* and the Anglo-Saxon word *boc*, which mean book, also mean the bark of a tree. And ancient people also engraved on tree leaves. Even now we call a page of a book a leaf. Therefore, we can call trees the beginning of the book. The following definition of literature by William Long considers the history of this origin and is very broad:[i] "Everything that the hand of man has written upon the tree or its products or its substitutes is literature."[3]

One might think that the scope of this definition is too broad and cannot explain completely the qualities of literature, but at least in one aspect it touches on the essence of literature. In one basic respect, literature is a written record. I will ask what kind of content is written and through what means later, but for now let us remember

---

[i] Long: *Outlines of English Literature*, p. 3.

the fact that literature is born through the attempt to write experience. Of course, there is a process of expression prior to a written record. However, the expression of experience naturally requires preservation. An experience that is not written cannot be preserved.

There will be countertheses to such a limiting of literature to a written record. Thomas De Quincey concludes that the book cannot be coextensive with the idea of literature, because not only are there many books that cannot be literature, but there are also literary things that are not books.[ii] If we call literature that is not a book *unwritten literature*, the examples that De Quincey gives of unwritten literature are lectures and, particularly, performances of plays that have literary content. However, there is no rule that lectures and speeches should not be written down. If they were not written down, then the reason was that the content was either valueless or incidental. We can also assign more efficacy to the performance of a play on stage than to a reading of the script, but it is reasonable to treat performance, as a theatrical art, differently from literature.

[ii] De Quincey: "Essay on The Works of Alexander Pope," *North British Review*, August 1848. This essay also appears in *The Art of Criticism*. This essay is easily confused with De Quincey's "Pope," which appears in volume 7 of the *Encyclopaedia Britannica*, but the two essays are totally distinct.

What we call oral literature presents a more difficult problem than De Quincey's counterargument and refers to literature that does not borrow the mediation of letters and that is transmitted from one mouth to another, such as classical epic poetry or medieval romances and ballads. Richard Moulton divides literature into fixed literature and current literature and treats oral literature as important, but it is a fact that the oral literature of Greece was almost all put into writing.[iii] If we imagine that *The Iliad* and *The Odyssey*[iv] were not put into writing by Homer's hand, that *Beowulf*[v] was not put into writing by some monk's hand, or that *Ossian*[vi] was not put into writing by James Macpherson's hand, then how would they remain today as literature? Of course, the research of scholars such as Moulton also could not have existed.

[iii] Moulton: *Modern Study of Literature*, chapter 2, section 2.

[iv] *The Iliad* and *The Odyssey* are works of the blind epic poet Homer, who is thought to have lived in Greece in the ninth century BC. They are called works, but they are not works in the contemporary sense. Legends of the Trojan War that singing poets had been transmitting orally for a long time were compiled and put into writing.

[v] *Beowulf* is a legend brought from Germany when the Anglo-Saxons entered England in the eighth century, but in the tenth century monks wrote down the legend, which scops had been singing for a long time. It is the oldest work of English literature.

[vi] In the case of *Ossian*, Macpherson put into verse (and published in 1763) a legend of a heroic Gaelic poet presumed to have lived in the third century; however, the majority of it was actually his creation. Beginning with Goethe, this poem influenced many of the Romantics.

It is a fact that even today, when writing has spread and printing has developed, many stories and songs that have not been put into writing are still in circulation here and there around the world. However, we do not call them literature but rather tradition. The reason is that they have not yet been given sufficient expression literarily. Among them there are also many that are magnificent as material for literature. However, they are still not literature.

When we ask concretely "What is literature?" we can only point to books. This is a fact that has special importance for people researching literature. Without books there cannot be literary research. Taking hints from literary works and analyzing life and criticizing life problems is interesting in relation to literary research, and a rich experience, but the object of literary research is always strictly concrete books.

2. Literature of Knowledge and Literature of Power

It is a fact that when we call a written record literature, the scale is too broad and is not particularly helpful for our research. Among these records are included books that give first consideration to facts and knowledge, such as mathematics books, collections of laws, and economic plans, as well as countless art books; these were called literature in Greece, but we call them documents and differentiate them from literature. Long's definition introduced above is also a definition of documents in the broad meaning, and not a definition of literature in the narrow meaning. If the scope of the definition is narrowed significantly, literature can be defined like this: "Literature is the written record of man's best thought and feeling . . . It excludes works which aim at instruction, and includes only the works which aim to give pleasure."[vii]

According to this definition, not only are documents excluded from literature, but among books in the humanities disciplines, the majority of publications in history, religion, philosophy, and ethics that give first consideration to knowledge and instruction would also fall outside of literature. Long differentiates literature and nonliterature by applying the standard of purpose, but we should think about the degree to which this differentiation is indeed appropriate. The purpose of literature is quite a complicated problem, and one can reference various sources that address it, but here I will first define the concept of literature itself and deal with it to the necessary degree.

Differentiating between literature and nonliterature according to the writer's teleology was a traditional

---

[vii] Long: *Outlines of English Literature*, p. 5.

mode of conventional criticism. However, because instruction and pleasure came to be opposed to each other in teleology after the classical era, the concept of literature, rather than being elucidated, was actually in a state that only created confusion. It is the basic position of this writer that the dispute between instruction and pleasure is a separate problem detached from the purpose of literature, and this position was actually a conclusion extrapolated from works rather than from some sort of theoretical basis. If next one considers various examples that are quickly and easily understood, then I believe one will be sympathetic with this position.

It is a fact that the scripts of Shakespeare, the lyric poetry of Wordsworth, and the prose of J. W. Goethe give pleasure to readers, but, on the other hand, it is also a fact that they illuminate some truths about life and provide deep instruction. In contrast, new scientific discoveries—for example, atomic power—give to scientists themselves and their readers feelings of astonishment and deep spiritual satisfaction, and it is clear that the pleasure of the results of the earliest analysis is essentially identical to artistic pleasure. Then are these scientific books literature?

I pointed out that De Quincey states that the idea of a book cannot be coextensive with the idea of literature, and of course this statement is meant to rigorously differentiate literature. With the same strictness he takes up the instruction/pleasure opposition and refuses to use it to distinguish between literature and nonliterature. He gives the example of Milton's *Paradise Lost* and asks the following:[4] "In which class of books does *Paradise Lost* stand? Among those which instruct, or those which *amuse*? Now, if a man answers, among those which instruct, he lies; for there is no instruction in it. . . . But if he says, 'no—amongst those which amuse,'—then what a beast he must be to degrade, and in this way, what has done the most of any human work to raise and dignify human nature."[viii]

De Quincey negates the commonsense dichotomy of "books for knowledge and books for pleasure." "Now, what is that antithesis to *knowledge*, which is here implicitly latent in the word literature? The vulgar antithesis is *pleasure* ('aut prodesse volunt, aut delectare poetae'). Books, we arc told, propose to *instruct* or to *amuse*. Indeed! However, not to spend any words upon it, I suppose you will admit that this wretched antithesis will be of no service to us."[ix]

[viii] De Quincey: "Letter to a Young Man Whose Education Has Been Neglected," *London Magazine*, March 1823. This essay appears in P. R. Lieder and R. Withington (Ed.): *The Art of Literary Criticism* (Appleton Century, 1941). The page number cited in the next note refers to this collection.

[ix] *Letters to a Young Man*, p. 440.

Instruction and pleasure were actually two traps that critics set for themselves, and they could not help but fall into them and then try to escape. If they escaped from one trap, they necessarily fell into the other. Until they eliminate these traps completely, literary critics will not be able to advance even a single step. By coming up with a new concept, De Quincey liberated himself from this bind. "The true antithesis to knowledge, in this case, is not *pleasure*, but *power*. All that is Literature seeks to communicate power; all that is not literature, to communicate knowledge."[x]

Concerning the question of what this power is that is the antithesis of knowledge, De Quincy describes, in a famous passage from his letters, the effects one receives from the final scene of *King Lear*, but there is no theoretical explanation. More than in this text, De Quincey responds to this question somewhat more concretely in "Essays on the Works of Alexander Pope," written twenty-five years later.[xi]

> In that great social organ, which, collectively, we call literature, there may be distinguished two separate offices that may blend and often *do* so, but capable, severally, of a severe insulation, and naturally fitted for reciprocal repulsion. There is, first, the literature of *knowledge*; and, secondly, the literature

---

[x] *Ibid.*, p. 441.
[xi] De Quincey: "Essay on The Works of Alexander Pope."

of *power*.[xii] The function of the first is—to *teach*; the function of the second is—to *move*: the first is a rudder; the second, an oar or a sail.[5]

For what purpose, then, and through what operation does literature move the human?

De Quincey calls the power of literature a "deep sympathy with truth." We do not learn anything new in *Paradise Lost*. Is it correct, then, to evaluate a cookbook more highly than *Paradise Lost*? Of course not. Why?

> What you owe to Milton is not knowledge, of which a million separate items are still but a million of advancing steps on the same earthly level; what you owe, is *power*, that is exercise and expansion to your own latent capacity of sympathy with the infinite, where every pulse and each separate influx is a step upwards—a step ascending as upon a Jacob's ladder from earth to mysterious altitudes above the earth. *All* the steps of knowledge, from first to last, carry you further on the same plane, but could never raise you one foot above your ancient level of earth: whereas, the very *first* step in power is a flight—is an ascending movement into another element where earth is forgotten.[xiii]

Because De Quincey is a Romantic critic, he used words such as "infinity" and "the world that opens when we forget the earth," but these words are the peculiar vocabulary of that time, indicating the world of art, and

---

[xii] In this essay, De Quincey uses the word *literature* rather than *book*. We can understand that the distinction between book and literature is not strict for him.
[xiii] *Essay on Pope* (*Art of Criticism*, p. 449).

there is no need to dwell on them deeply. More than that, there is a need to pay attention to how he explains the operation of the power of literature.

> The first (the literature of knowledge) speaks to the *mere* discursive understanding; the second (the literature of power) speaks ultimately, it may happen, to the higher understanding or reason, but always *through* feelings of pleasure and sympathy. Remotely, it may travel towards an object seated in what Lord Bacon calls *dry* light; but, proximately, it does and must operate, else it ceases to be a literature of *power*, on and through that *humid* light which clothes itself in the mists and glittering *iris* of human passions, desires, and genial emotions.[xiv]

3. Science and Literature

De Quincey viewed literature mainly in its functional aspect, but the distinction between literature and science certainly becomes clear in his definition. De Quincey did not use the word *science*, but it is clear that "books of knowledge" refer mainly to science. When we view Isaac Newton's *Mathematical Principles of Natural Philosophy* and Shakespeare's scripts together, between science, which teaches knowledge, and literature, which moves us, there exists a distinction we can suitably recognize. However, there is a field in the middle of them that extends in both directions. It includes, for example, philosophy such as

---

[xiv] *Ibid.*, p. 448.

Blaise Pascal's *Penseés*, history such as Edward Gibbon's *The History of the Decline and Fall of the Roman Empire*, and the political theses of Edmund Burke. Even though their content is made up of facts and knowledge, these works have an enormous power to move readers. Are they literature? Are they science? If we can put them in the category of literature, what is the basis for doing so?

Now let us look at an opposite example. Works whose main topics are knowledge and thought have traditionally been referred to as nonliterature and have been ignored, but contemporary intellectualist literature is characterized by antiemotionalism and a respect for the truth. This sort of literary attitude appeared in enacting a reevaluation of classical literature and giving new significance to the poets of natural philosophy in Greece, the poets of sonnets in the Italian Middle Ages, and the poets of philosophical movements in seventeenth-century England. When observing such a phenomenon, one can understand that subject matter is not the only thing that differentiates science and literature. If subject matter does not differentiate them, then the clues to a resolution can only be discovered within the methods of treating the subject matter.

Those who theorize the difference between science and art commonly argue that science deals with truth and art deals with beauty. In literary theory the same confusion emerged. This was a trap that interrupted the progress of literary criticism, as was the binary of instruction and pleasure.

Walter Pater was the one who cleared up a lot of confusion, while personally treading across a land with many dangers: the area between two realms.[xv] Even while departing from the identical questions as De Quincey, he goes a little deeper and offers somewhat clearer ideas. "The essential dichotomy in this matter, between imaginative and unimaginative writing, parallel to De Quincey's distinction between 'the literature of power' and 'the literature of knowledge,' [is that] in the former . . . the composer gives us not fact, but his peculiar sense of fact."[xvi]

Pater's fundamental idea is that literature, too, like science, is primarily concerned with facts. However, in science facts are expressed as facts, but literature expresses a specific way of understanding facts—imaginative understanding. If we refer to science as a transcription of facts, literature is a transcription of the understanding of facts. We could even call it a certain spiritual transcription of facts. How so?

[xv] The place where Walter Pater treated this problem is "Style." This essay takes the difference between prose and poetry as its primary topic, but it includes important discussions about the foundations of literature. It appears in *Appreciations with An Essay on Style* (Macmillan, 1942).
[xvi] *Appreciations*, p. 7.

Let us think about history, for example. When an editor of a chronicle records as is the historical facts that appeared in a certain period and manufactures a chronology, this is a transcription of facts in the strict sense. However, when a historian writes history under a definitive historical viewpoint, this cannot remain only a transcription of facts. First of all, the writer must choose their materials among innumerable facts, and these choices are determined by the perspective they take on the historical world. Another term for perspective is imaginative intuition. Next they provide their own interpretation of the facts that they have chosen, and this interpretation is connected to the single soul referred to as the individuality of the historian—their disposition, will, and life view. The facts that are expressed in a history book are not facts at their core but facts that live in the soul of the historian. Things are already tinged with the unique tones in the historian's imagination. If so, then the transcription is already approaching art. "Just in proportion as the writer's aim, consciously or unconsciously, comes to be the transcribing, not of the world, not of mere fact, but of his sense of it, he becomes an artist, his work, *fine* art."[xvii]

If we apply this statement to literature, then ultimately the argument is the same and goes as follows. "Literary

---

[xvii] *Ibid.* p. 9.

art, that is, like all art which is in any way imitative or reproductive of fact—form, or color, or incident—is the representation of such fact as connected with soul, of a specific personality, in its preferences, its volition and power. Such is the matter of imaginative or artistic literature—this transcript, not of mere fact, but of fact in its infinite variety, as modified by human preference in all its infinitely varied forms."[xviii]

The truth that appears in infinitely varied forms—we call this beauty. This is why beauty is often conflated with truth in literature. "As in those humbler or plainer functions of literature also, truth—truth to bare fact, there—is the essence of such artistic quality as they may have. Truth! There can be no merit, no craft at all, without that. And further, all beauty is in the long run only *fineness* of truth, or what we call expression, the finer accommodation of speech to that vision within."[xix]

4. A Record of Valuable Experience

Through the definitions of De Quincey and Pater, the scope of literature becomes smaller and, its concept becomes much clearer. Now let us try to offer a definition

---

[xviii] *Ibid.*, p. 10.
[xix] *Ibid.*, p. 10.

that delimits the concept of literature directly. I will begin by repeating Long's definition.

> "Literature is the written record of man's best thought
> and feeling."—Long
> "Literature is an expression of the best of thought."—
> Ralph Waldo Emerson[xx]
> "By letters of literature is meant the expression of
> thought in language, where by 'thought' I mean the
> ideas, feelings, views, reasonings, and other opera-
> tions of the human mind."—John Henry Newman[xxi]

If we combine the above definitions, we get the following. "Literature is an expression or record, by means
of language, of the best thoughts and feelings of the
human." Expression? Record? Because expression by
means of language concretely refers to a written record,
either term works. However, for the same reason that I
cited before, let us use the word *record*. Doing so does not
mean attaching no great significance to the process of expression in literature. On the contrary, I would even con-
jecture that expression practically makes up the whole
of literature.

[xx] Quoted in Caleb Thomas Winchester: *Some Principles of Literary
Criticism*, p. 36.
[xxi] Newman: *Idea of the University*, p. 291.

I plan to write a separate text in the future concerning expression and explain in more detail, but here I will just emphasize the fact that expression combines thought and emotion. De Quincey's idea of literature eventually arrived at dry reason, but first De Quincey stated that it operates only through "the wet sunbeams, between the fog and the brilliant iris, of human sentiment, passion, and desire" or "the emotions of pleasure and sympathy," and Pater argued that objective facts "are colored by the imagination and radiate distinctive hues" only through the individuality of the author and that these facts "appear modified by personal preference in all its infinitely varied forms." These are all characteristics of the operation of the spirit called expression. Literature does not treat thought and emotion abstractly and analytically like science; it treats them concretely and synthetically. Thought and emotion do not move separately within us. They are always a vital process moving organically, as a whole, one as the cause and the other as the effect. We call this vital process experience. I define literature, then, as a record of human experience.

Whether literary research can become science is an important question, but if literary research is permitted to treat experience abstractly and analytically, of course it will become science. However, the vitality of literary research will at the same time die. Here lies the anxiety of literary researchers. How can one grasp literary vitality as is in scientifically strict descriptions? That is the largest agony this author has in writing this book. No matter how difficult it is, I promise to put forward my full effort to try to observe and explain literature through experience.

What does it mean that Long and Emerson refer to "the *best* thought and emotion" in their definitions? Why must the thought and emotion of literature be the best? Is it that the finest and the best are problems within criticism that have nothing to do with the creation of literature? Not only is it baseless for a writer to think of themselves as the best, but even if a writer thinks they are the best, if society does not recognize them as such, then isn't that the extent of it? Isn't including this sort of uncertain condition in the definition of literature irrational? I know that innumerable questions and objections like this will be posed. Even so, let us preserve this condition as the most important condition in the definition of literature.

In my thinking, the idea of a written record is the most fundamental idea of literature. In other words, the will to preserve is the motivation and the driving force of literary creation. If so, then it is reasonable that the thoughts and emotions treated in literature must be the best and the finest to that person. They must be so because no person would try to preserve something without value. Opposing mediocrity in form or in content is almost instinctual in literature. Horace states, "[M]ediocrity has been banned by Gods, people, and bookstore owners alike." There is a further problem, in that this kind of subjective self-evaluation must agree with objective criticism, but that is not an issue to discuss here. They can agree or not agree. And what is called objective criticism also differs according to era. However, because it is a certain fact that a writer will only come to have the will to express when they think that their own thoughts and emotions have value and are worthy of preservation for future generations, before writing they must adopt a formed feeling of value as one condition for the definition of literature. Therefore, the definition of literature is modified as follows: "Literature is a valuable record of human experience."

There are cases to be excluded from this definition. For example, the case of the hack writer who has no serious evaluation of their own thoughts and emotions and carelessly writes something. This is a problem related to human authenticity rather than to literature. Because this scenario is excluded from the fundamental idea of literature, the writing produced is nonliterature. There is no need in literary research, which has many tasks, to expend one's mind on nonliterature.

5. Opposite Extremes of the Idea of Literature

When we examine the innumerable definitions[xxii] of literature expressed in the past, what surprises us is that
there are so many different definitions concerning the
same literature. Next let us introduce two definitions
that stand at opposite extremes:

> "Every great piece of literature, without any excep-
> tion, is an assertion of moral law, as strict as the Eu-
> menides or the *Divina Commedia*."—John Ruskin[xxiii]
>
> "Literature we call any structure in language which
> is fine art. Its characteristic excellence is literary
> beauty."—Harold Osborne[xxiv]

One is the definition of a nineteenth-century critic, and
the other is a definition of a contemporary aesthetician.
Putting these two definitions at opposite extremes, we
can enumerate samples such as the following:

[xxii] Among the definitions that are not introduced here, some that
deserve attention can be found in the following books: J. Morley, *On the
Study of Literature*, pp. 39–40; Hutcheson Macaulay Posnett, *Comparative
Literature*, p. 18; Edward Dowden, *Transcripts and Studies*, pp. 237–40;
Henry Nettleship, *The Moral Influence of Literature*; Lucius Adelno Sher-
man, *The Analytics of Literature*, chapter 1; John Bascom, *Philosophy of
English Literature*, lecture 1; Thomas Arnold, *Manual of English Literature*,
pp. 341–42; George Henry Lewes, *Principles of Success in Literature*, chap-
ter 1; Hamilton Wright Mabie, *Short Studies in Literature*, p. 5; Brother
Azarius, *The Philosophy of Literature*.

[xxiii] Ruskin: *Fors Clavigera*, volume 4, letter 73.

[xxiv] Osborne: *Aesthetics and Criticism*, p. 260.

"Literature is the expression in letters of the spiritual, cooperating with the intellectual, man, the former being the primary, dominant coefficient."—Hiram Corson[xxv]

"By literature we mean the written thoughts and feelings of intelligent men and women, arranged in a way that shall give pleasure to the reader."—Stopford Brooke[xxvi]

"Literature is composed of those books, and of those books only, which, in the first place, by reason of their subject-matter and their mode of treating it, are of general human interest; and in which, in the second place, the element of form and the pleasure which form gives are to be regarded as essential."—William Henry Hudson[xxvii]

Therefore, the fact that we cannot have a singular definition originates in the qualities of literature itself—the multifaceted expression of experience. It is a fact that definitions will differ according to the position from which we view literature. Because literature is a type of art, we can observe it by dividing its form and its content to a certain degree. If we ignore the side of content and abstract the formal components, the concept we will arrive at in the end is language as expressive mediation. Therefore, literature can be delimited as the art of language.

[xxv] Corson: *The Aims of Literary Study*, p. 24.

[xxvi] Brooke: *Primer of English Literature*, p. 5.

[xxvii] Hudson: *An Introduction to the Study of Literature*, p. 12.

The German term *Wortkunst* (language art) is a techni-
cal term that indicates this concept directly. Language
art has the advantage of including oral literature that is
not recorded, and aestheticians favor it because they can
do comparative research on identical aspects that literature shares with the plastic and sound arts, but even in
Germany it is not generally used, because it excessively
simplifies the idea of literature.

In stating that the innate superiority in literature is its
beauty, the formal components are too vague and, on the
other hand, the intellectual components in the content—
thoughts and morals—are onerous. If we cannot apply
an arbitrary generalization to literature, which has this
double-sided nature, then we cannot form a theory of
literature that is partial to only one of these sides. Furthermore, in literature, thought and morals are not, as
the aestheticist thinks, either exotic or ancillary. Even if
we do not go so far as to think, like Ruskin, that literature is the assertion of moral law, we can understand
why thought and morals are not exotic or ancillary if we
consider the qualities of language, which is the medium
of expression of literature. The intellectual material of
literature is limited to being one part of the meaning that
language itself contains. Therefore, so-called language
art is an innate attribute that cannot be discarded obsti-
nately in determining if thought or morals are good or

bad. In the future I will publish a separate text examining from a new angle the meaning of language in relation to the content of literature, but in any case, there I will declare that I will not take part in a theory of language art that attempts to consider literature by the sole standard of beauty. In this sense, Hudson's definition seems to be plain and to have no novelty, but it is a definition of literature that we can be comfortable with and rely on.

It is a fact that the character of art is determined by its medium of expression, but we cannot deny that art is also, after all, a product of the artist's spirit. Views of art can differ fundamentally according to whether we see the human in the background of art as purely an artist or also as a moralist. The Greeks called poets *poiētēs* and clearly recognized the word's technician-like character; however, on the other hand, because they insisted strongly that the object of poetic imitation was in all respects the acting human—or the moral person—their poems transcended the scope of mere *tekne* (making) and were *sophia* (wisdom). In the Roman era, poets were *vates* (soothsayers), during the Renaissance they were humanists, and there was no disruption of these traditions into the nineteenth century. The betrayal of these traditions began with aestheticism at the end of the nineteenth century. Summarizing and speaking for the perspective of literary arts from that era onward, and equating poetry with bridge building, Joel Elias Spingarn writes the following: "It is not the inherent function of poetry to further any moral or social cause, any more than it is the function of bridge-building to further the cause of Esperanto."[xxviii] Equating poetry with music and architecture, he states, "To say that poetry, as poetry, is moral or immoral is as meaningless as to say that an equilateral triangle is moral and an isosceles triangle immoral, or to speak of the immorality of a musical chord or a Gothic arch."[xxix] A sound reader will not approve at all of this kind of extreme theory. In contrast to viewing as proper Hudson's definition, which states that the formal element is the essential element in literature, Corson demarcating litterateurs as intellectuals is something deeply meaningful. I think that his demand to poets that they become thinkers and moralists is unreasonable, but I agree with Matthew Arnold that because poets always research how human beings should live, poetry itself is the criticism of life.[xxx]

[xxviii] Spingarn: "The New Criticism," *American Critical Essays, XIX–XX Century*, ed. by Norman Foerster (World's Classics), pp. 442–43.

[xxix] *Ibid.*, p. 443.

[xxx] Arnold: Preface to *Poems of Wordsworth*, 1870. Because Arnold has three writings with similar titles, it is easy to confuse them. (1) Preface to *Poems of Matthew Arnold*, 1853. This essay was later republished in *Irish Essays*. (2) Preface to *Poems of Wordsworth*, 1870. (3) General introduction to *The English Poets*, ed. by T. H. Wards, 1880. It was later included in *Essays in Criticism: Second Series* under the title "The Study of Poetry."

6. The Methods of Research

Should all literary research stop at appreciation? Or should it go further and become scholarship? Discussing these questions in detail is a difficult problem involving philosophical consideration, and I will postpone it for a book I have planned, *Introduction to Literary Research Methods*; here I will summarize the gist of the method employed in this book.

This theory describes as theoretically and systematically as possible the literary phenomena that are considered important. The object treated here is literary experience, which includes many irrational elements, but this theory itself must be a system of knowledge. Because only experience as vital process is a mutual operation of environment and organism, only it has the double-sidedness of subject and object. If we abstract excessively for the purpose of systemizing knowledge, its content becomes empty. This kind of pedantic thinking should be prohibited as much as possible.

This theory is not satisfied with only describing literary phenomena, and it goes a step further and tries to explain these phenomena. Explanation is already a scientific method. Literature is a record of experience, and because experience is a single process of arriving at a single effect from a single cause, literature can be explained scientifically. Through such an explanation, we can dispense with the many mystical theories that have hitherto pushed outside of our understanding the theories of literature that can grasp the works and phenomena of literature, and thereby we can make literature into a thing that can be understood to a degree.

First, of course I do not think that literature can be dealt with and explained scientifically from beginning to end. The individuality and genius of the most important authors in literature and the uniqueness of the works that appear in it cannot be explained scientifically. What cannot be explained scientifically we can only experience directly. In this sense, thinking of literature as science must be abandoned.

Second, if scientific explanations of literature are to try to attain satisfactory results, then they must borrow the power of auxiliary sciences—and particularly among them psychology and linguistics—but these sciences are all still in a state of incompletion. In this book, the psychology of William James, John Dewey, and I. A. Richards were employed,[xxxi] but their psychological studies also leave many unresolved questions. Semantics, which has recently appeared in the field of linguistics, gives us

---

[xxxi] James: *Psychology*, 1887; Dewey: *Art as Experience*, 1934; Richards: *Principles of Literary Criticism*, 1924.

a lot of hope, but it seems it will still require appropriate time if it is going to make any substantive contribution to the criticism and research of literature.

The uniqueness and irrationality of literature, which cannot be explained scientifically, can be grasped to some degree through what Benedetto Croce calls historical method.[xxxii] For example, we see that each era wanders almost cyclically between the view that the function of literature is instruction and the view that it is pleasure, and we can state that the rhythm that emerges from this literary movement and countermovement is itself the essence of literature. In considering this problem, we cannot establish a fixed generalization that chooses one side. This phenomenon can be understood through historical explanation. In this book I often employ historical explanation in this sense.

Rather than clarifying the idea of literature, the above enumeration of definitions has probably introduced many problems and created more confusion. However, isn't the purpose of definitions to provide a point of departure for speculation and to point to the location of problems? Here we will consider all the problems that have been introduced and suggested, and later I will return again to definitions.

[xxxii] Croce: *History: Its Theory and Practice*, 1921.

Notes by the Editor

1. For translating "The Idea of Literature," I referred to the version published in Ch'oe, "Munhak."

2. Both "literature" and "letters" appear in English in the original.

3. Ch'oe's footnotes are included. In the original essay, many of these footnotes contained English-language quotations that Ch'oe translated into Korean in the body of the essay. I have used these quotations in my own translation, checking Ch'oe's transcription of the English when sources were available. The English quotations have been removed from the footnotes.

4. I have referenced De Quincey, *Letters* 84, for this quotation, which appears in English in Ch'oe's original footnote.

5. I have referenced De Quincey, "Alexander Pope" 5. Ch'oe adds one sentence to the quotation that does not appear in the original text by De Quincey. The sentence now follows the quotation.

WORKS CITED IN NOTES BY THE EDITOR

Arnold, Matthew. *Culture and Anarchy*. Oxford UP, 2006.

Butcher, S. H., translator. *Poetics*. By Aristotle, Dover, 1951.

Ch'oe Chaesŏ. "교양의 정신" ["Kyoyang ŭi chŏngsin"; "The Spirit of Cultivation"]. 인문평론 [*Inmun p'yŏngnon; Humanities Critique*], vol. 2, Nov. 1939, pp. 24–29.

———. "문학의 이상" ["Munhak ŭi isang"; "The Idea of Literature"]. 문학원론 [*Munhak wŏllon; Literary Theory*], Ch'unjosa, 1957, pp. 1–16.

———. "何が詩的であるか" ["Nani ga shiteki de aru ka"; "What Is Poetic?"]. 転換期の朝鮮文学 [*Tenkanki no Chōsen bungaku; Korean Literature in a Time of Transition*], Jinbunsha, 1943, pp. 181–86.

De Quincey, Thomas. "Alexander Pope." *De Quincey's Works*, vol. 8, Adam and Charles Black, 1862, pp. 1–53.

———. *Letters of De Quincey, the English Opium-Eater, to a Young Man Whose Education Has Been Neglected*. John Penington, 1843.

Desmarets de Saint-Sorlin, Jean. *Rosane, histoire tirée de celles des Romains et des Perses* [*Rosane: A Story Based on Those of the Romans and Persians*]. Le Gras, 1639.

Hegel, G. W. F. *Hegel's Aesthetics: Lectures on Fine Art*. Translated by T. M. Knox, vol. 1, Oxford UP, 1998.

———. *The Philosophy of History*. Translated by J. Sibree, Dover, 1956.

Heidegger, Martin. *Being and Time*. Translated by John Macquarrie and Edward Robinson, Blackwell, 1962.

Im Hwa. "My Brother and the Brazier." Translated by Jiwon Shin. *Columbia Anthology of Modern Korean Poetry*, Columbia UP, 2004, pp. 41–44.

———. "우리 오빠와 화로" ["Uri oppa wa hwaro"; "My Brother and the Brazier"]. 시 [*Si; Poems*], Somyŏng, 2009, pp. 56–57. Vol. 1 of 임화문학예술전집 [*Im Hwa munhak yesul chŏnjip; The Complete Literary Art of Im Hwa*].

———. "유월 중의 창작" ["Yuwŏl chung ŭi ch'angjak"; "Creative Writing from June"]. 평론1 [*P'yŏngnon 1; Criticism 1*], Somyŏng, 2009, pp. 246–68. Vol. 4 of 임화문학예술전집 [*Im Hwa munhak yesul chŏnjip; The Complete Literary Art of Im Hwa*].

Kōyama Iwao. 文化類型學研究 [*Bunka ruikeigaku kenkyū; Research on the Typology of Culture*]. Kōbundō, 1941.

Krojzl, Clare, translator. *A History of German Literature: From the Beginnings to the Present Day*. Edited by Wolfgang Beutin et al., Routledge, 2005.

Lau, D. C., translator. *The Analects*. By Confucius, Penguin, 1979.

———, translator. *Tao Te Ching*. By Lao Tzu, Penguin, 1963.

Legge, James, translator and editor. *The Doctrine of the Mean*, by Zisi. *The Chinese Classics: With a Translation, Critical and Exegetical Notes, Prolegomena, and Copious Indexes*. Vol. 1, Trübner, 1861, pp. 382–434.

Lough, William, translator. "The German Ideology." By Karl Marx. *Karl Marx and Friedrich Engels Collected Works, 1845–1847*. Vol. 5, International Publishers, 1976.

Nabe, Clyde, translator. "On the Idea of Man." By Max Scheler. *Journal of the British Society for Phenomenology*, vol. 9, no. 3, Oct. 1978, pp. 184–98.

Ŏm Hosŏk. "문학 창작에 있어서의 전형성의 문제" ["Munhak ch'angjak e issŏsŏ ŭi chŏnhyŏngsŏng ŭi munje"; "The Problem of Typicality in Literary Creation"]. 문학의 지향 [*Munhak ŭi chihyang; The Aims of Literature*], edited by An Hamgwang, Chosŏn Chakka Tongmaeng, 1954, pp. 128–43.

Paik Ch'ŏl. "자연주의 뒤에 올 것—외적 인간과 심리계의 통일" ["Chayŏnjuŭi twi e ol kŏt—oejŏk in'gan kwa simnigye ŭi t'ongil"; "What Comes after Naturalism: The Unity of the External Human and the Psychological World"]. 문학예술 [*Munhak yesul; Literary Arts*], vol. 3, no. 1, 1956, pp. 116–22.

———. "자연주의의 극복을 위하여—전통과 인간에 쏟아지는 애정으로" ["Chayŏnjuŭi ŭi kŭkpok ŭl wihayŏ—chŏnt'ong kwa in'gan e ssodajinŭn aejŏng ŭro"; "Toward the Overcoming of Naturalism: Through a Love of Tradition and the Human"]. 백철평론 선집 [*Paik Ch'ŏl p'yŏngnon sŏnjip; The Selected Criticism of Paik Ch'ŏl*], edited by Yi Sŭngha, Chisik ŭl Mandŭnŭn Chisik, 2015, pp. 173–86.

———. "인간묘사시대" ["In'gan myosa sidae"; "The Era of Human Description"]. 조선일보 [*Chosŏn ilbo; The Chosun Ilbo*], 29 Aug.–1 Sept. 1933. 조선 뉴스 라이브러리 [*Chosŏn nyusŭ raibŭrŏri; Chosun News Library*], newslibrary.chosun.com.

———. "삼천만인의 문학—민중은 어떤 문학을 요망하는가" ["Samch'ŏnman in ŭi munhak—minjung ŭn ŏttŏn munhak ŭl yomang hanŭn'ga"; "Literature for Thirty Million Koreans: What Kind of Literature Do the People Desire?"]. 문학 [*Munhak; Literature*], May 1950, pp. 120–25.

Sakai, Naoki. *Translation and Subjectivity: On "Japan" and Cultural Nationalism.* U of Minnesota P, 1997.

Sŏ Insik. "지성의 시대적 성격" ["Chisŏng ŭi sidaejŏk sŏnggyŏk"; "The Timely Character of the Intellect"]. 역사와 문화 [*Yŏksa wa munhwa; History and Culture*], edited by Ch'a Sŭnggi and Chŏng Chonghyŏn, Yŏngnak, 2006, pp. 96–113. Vol. 1 of 서인식전집 [*Sŏ Insik chŏnjip; Sŏ Insik Complete Works*].

———. "'향수'의 사회학" ["'Hyangsu' ŭi sahoehak"; "Sociology of 'Nostalgia'"]. 조광 [*Chogwang; Morning Light*], vol. 6, no. 11, 1940, pp. 182–89.

———. "문학과 윤리" ["Munhak kwa yulli"; "Literature and Ethics"]. 인문평론 [*Inmun p'yŏngnon; Humanities Critique*], vol. 2, no. 10, 1940, pp. 6–22.

———. 신문 · 잡지편 [*Sinmun · chapchip'yŏn; Newspaper and Journal Articles*]. Edited by Ch'a Sŭnggi and Chŏng Chonghyŏn, Yŏngnak, 2006. Vol. 2 of 서인식전집 [*Sŏ Insik chŏnjip; Sŏ Insik Complete Works*].

———. "동양문화의 이념과 형태—그 특수성과 일반성" ["Tongyang
munhwa ŭi inyŏm kwa hyŏngt'ae—kŭ t'ŭksusŏng kwa ilbansŏng";
"The Idea and Form of Eastern Culture: Its Particularity and Generality"]. 동아일보 [*Tonga ilbo; The Dong-a Ilbo*], 3–12 Jan. 1940.

Watsuji Tetsurō. 人間学としての倫理学 [*Ningengaku to shite no rinrigaku;
Ethics as Philosophical Anthropology*]. Iwanami Shoten, 2007.

ABOUT THE EDITOR

Travis Workman is associate professor in the Department of Asian and Middle Eastern Studies at the University of Minnesota, Twin Cities. He is the author of *Imperial Genus: The Formation and Limits of the Human in Modern Korea and Japan* (2015).